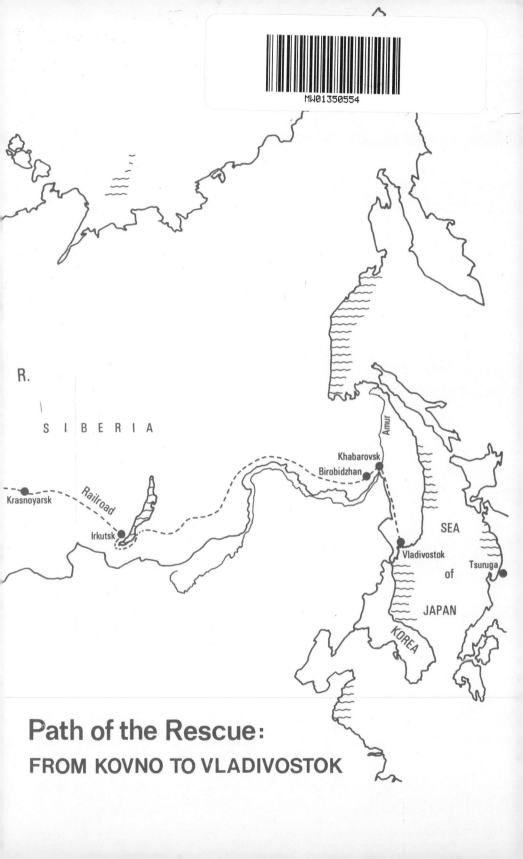

OPERATION: TORAH RESCUE

N° 41.

Le Consulat des Pays-Bas à Kaunas déclare par la présente que pour l'admission d'étrangers au Surinam, au Curaçao et autres possessions néerlandaises en Amérique un visa d'entrée n'est pas requis.

Kaunas, le 24 juillet 1940

Consul des Pays-Bas a.i.

TRANSIT-VI

Seen for the through Japan (to Curaçao and othe lands' colonies.)

Japan

YECHESKEL LEITNER

Operation:
TORAH RESCUE

the escape of
the Mirrer Yeshiva
from war-torn Poland
to Shanghai, China

FELDHEIM PUBLISHERS
Jerusalem • New York

First published 1987
Hardcover edition: ISBN 0-87306-436-4
Paperback editon: ISBN 0-87306-441-0

Copyright © 1987 by Yecheskel Leitner

All rights reserved.
No part of this publication may be translated,
reproduced, stored in a retrieval system or transmitted,
in any form or by any means, electronic, photocopying,
recording or otherwise, without prior permission
in writing from the publishers.

Philipp Feldheim Inc.
200 Airport Executive Park
Spring Valley, NY 10977

Feldheim Publishers Ltd.
POB 6525 / Jerusalem, Israel

Printed in Israel

*This book is dedicated
to the memory of
unforgettable parents and guides in Jewish living*

ר' צבי ב"ר יחזקאל ז"ל

and

מרת רבקה שרה בת ר' יוסף ז"ל

to their constant aspirations in the service of the
Almighty and their unbending eagerness
to implant such goals
into the lives of their children.

---

*In remembrance of the distinguished founders
and Roshey Yeshiva
of Beth Hatalmud, New York*
Hagaon Harav Aryeh Leib Malin זצ"ל

and

Hagaon Harav Chaim Vysoker זצ"ל
whose planning, strength and wisdom of Torah
were the initiative and moral propellant of
the Mirrer Yeshiva students. Throughout the
turbulence of the rescue, they bore the
burden of the decisions and the awesome moral
responsibility for the lives and historic
mission of this elite Torah group.

THE REMEMBRANCE SERIES

A special collection of works that chronicle the survival of our People and our Faith throughout the war years.

Editorial Adviser
Rabbi Nachman Bulman

CONTENTS

Forward	5
Preface	7
Introduction	10
The Religious Faith of Polish Jewry	13
The Mitzva of the Esrog	18
Poland's Torah Centers Begin to Move	21
Profile of a Miracle	23
Lithuanian Jews — Embodiment of Torah and Chessed	27
Trapped Again	32
The Soviet Deportation Trap	35
The Greatest Folly	37
The NKVD Under Siege	40
The Advice of Torah	43
Leaving Russia For — Nowhere	46
For Two Lit	53
Under Duress	54
The Palm Reader	56
"On Eagles' Wings"	60

When Orthodox Rabbis Desecrated the Sabbath	62
Visiting Friends in Moscow	64
From Vilna to Vladivostok with Torah Luminaries	67
A New Hunger in a Hungry Land	70
Vladivostok	75
A Narrow Escape from Shipwreck	78
Japanese Hospitality	81
An Encounter with Idols and Idol Worship	85
The Japanese and the Ten Lost Tribes	87
The Free Port of Shanghai	90
War Expanding to the Far East	100
Esrogim in China	108
Japan and the "Final Solution"	111
Law and Punishment the Japanese Way	118
The Power of Intensive Torah Study	120
Traces of Idolatry in the Twentieth Century	125
The Last Battles of World War II	128
Efforts to Save Torah Scholars	134
In Review	137
In Perspective: The Fuehrer and the Anti-Fuehrer	140
Fulfillment	143
Glossary	149
Maps	152

FOREWORD
by Rabbi Nachman Bulman
editorial adviser for
The Remembrance Series

There are times when God chooses to disclose his Presence: the Exodus, Sinai, the Beis Hamikdash, Prophecy, miracles.

There are times when the Divine Countenance is hidden from view: Israel in Exile; the suffering of the righteous; the prosperity of the wicked; the People of the Torah turned to ashes, lampshades and soap.

There are times when Prophets and Sages help us read the handwriting of Divine Providence clearly. In the absence of Prophets, however, our ability to decipher that handwriting diminishes. In these times, the character and destiny of the Jewish People seem frighteningly uncertain.

Yet within the blur and confusion of alternating patterns of light and dark, of revealed and concealed Providence, one image remains sharply in focus: the presence of a Divine shield which protects — even in the very bowels of evil — some of those who, through their scholarship and guidance, would later help effect the resurrection of Torah and Nation, and some of those who, through the recounting of their experience, would become crucial instruments for a newly perceived Providence.

Thus it was with Moshe; thus with Yosef; thus with Daniel and his friends; thus with Esther. And thus in Hitler's Europe, through a convoluted set of circumstances no less complex than the events which cast Moshe, Yosef, Daniel and Esther in the role of the Almighty's chosen messenger for His People's deliverance.

In defiance of all rational explanation, within the all-encompassing power of Hitler's and Stalin's hell, a provision was made to protect and liberate some of the greatest Torah luminaries of the Old World. Their impact has virtually transformed the face of World Jewry.

Along with these esteemed scholars, a handful of our brothers and sisters survived, charged with the duty to remember and retell all they had witnessed: in Poland, in Hungary, in Siberia, in every part of the globe where the grasping hand of Satan reached.

An inestimable debt of gratitude is owed to the authors of these works. To read the amazing accounts of their salvation is to see, beyond all possibility of denial, that

נצח ישראל לא ישקר

the Eternal One of Israel does not fail.

Preface

אהללה שם אלקים בשיר — ואגדלנו בתודה.
*I will praise God's name with song
and exalt Him with thanksgiving.*
(PSALMS 69:31)

The dust that was raised during the Biblical struggle of Jacob with the angel of Esau-Edom will not settle until the end of time! Jacob emerged the victor, his Divinely ordained mission reconfirmed. The price he paid for this victory was a slight limp, a physical injury, from which he soon recovered. But to this day his descendants, the Jewish people, are not permitted to partake of meat that corresponds to the "dislocated sinew." This Biblical prohibition serves as a perpetual reminder of Jacob's miraculous rescue in this eternal combat.

The following saga of the rescue of *Torah** and groups of its scholars from the Holocaust is but another episode in this constant struggle throughout history. Aware of the historical dimensions of these events and grateful to the Almighty for His grace during the six-year trek from Europe to the U.S.A. via the Baltic states, Russia, Japan and China, I feel it incumbent upon myself to retell some of the historic events of this Torah rescue from the Holocaust and to share them with as wide an audience as possible.

---

* Note to the reader:
Italicized words which are not defined in the text are explained in the Glossary.

In this presentation, the author often relied upon the analytical evaluations of the *mashgiach* of the Mirrer Yeshiva, Rabbi Yechezkel Levenstein, of blessed memory. In lectures before the student body, he regularly presented his profound analyses of the historical phenomena encountered in the path of rescue. His approach to the variety of these experiences — as the students and scholars on their "Ark of Torah" were miraculously guided through the stormiest waters in Jewish history — gave rich meaning to events, deepened one's insight into their significance, raised morale above the pitfalls of ongoing hardship, and brought awareness of the overall historic context of those happenings.

I wish to thank the following friends and experts for their encouragement, advice and suggestions: Yehoshua Leiman, editor of *Light* magazine, who gave me invaluable advice and guidance in the publication of this book and who greatly improved the editorial content of the original manuscript; Professor David Kranzler, author of *Japanese, Nazis and Jews*; Rabbi Kasryel Orbach, author of *Pathways of Life*; and Rabbi Joseph D. Epstein, former secretary of the Mirrer Yeshiva, who graciously supplied some of the documentary picture material.

A note of acknowledgment and gratitude goes to my dedicated brother, R. Ben Zion Leitner, for bestowing much diligent effort on this book. He spent a great deal of time in critically scrutinizing the entire manuscript in order to impart his valuable advice and many practical suggestions regarding the organization of the material.

A final note of thanks to my devoted wife, Sara, for her encouragement and many valuable suggestions.

The author's basic approach to, and ability to absorb and digest these historic developments were molded by the outlook and attitudes, sacrifices and guidance of his parents. Their death by martyrdom was not only the culmination of their life but also embodied the very essence of their spiritual endeavors through a lifetime filled with rich Jewish spirituality.

This book, therefore, is dedicated to their memory, to their constant aspirations in the service of the Almighty and their unflagging eagerness to imbue such goals in their children. May their children's and grandchildren's aspirations and actions be a meaningful continuation of their ideals.

Yecheskel Leitner
Brooklyn, New York

Introduction

Throughout the history of the Jewish people, the outstanding teachers of Torah and Talmud were often heads of famous yeshivos, academies of Jewish learning. This was true particularly in Russia, Poland and Lithuania, where famous yeshivos brought the study of Torah to the richest fruition.

One of Europe's "Ivy League" yeshivos was the Yeshiva of Mir, founded in 1817. The township of Mir (the name means "peace" in Russian) was located in a remote corner of Poland, near the eastern border with Russia. As the seat of the Mirrer Yeshiva, this *shtetl* was transformed by the varied national origins of the students into an international community of sorts. Here, the most promising Torah minds gathered to immerse themselves in Torah knowledge at the highest level attainable among yeshivos of the day. Jewish students flocked to the Mirrer Yeshiva from all over the globe, not only from Poland, Russia, and Lithuania, but also from France, Germany and Sweden, from England, America, and even South Africa. In fact, Rabbi Abraham Kalmanowitz, the dean of the Mirrer Yeshiva in America — where it was transplanted following its miraculous escape during World War II — once remarked in a lighter vein that the only nationality not represented in the student body of the Mirrer Yeshiva was China. "That," he said, "was the reason why the Yeshiva had to go to Shanghai," where it was stranded for five years on its escape route from the Holocaust.

When the famous Torah institution arrived in the United States in 1946, the city of New York accorded the members an official welcome, including the presentation of the "Key to the City," an honor bestowed only on outstanding dignitaries and world leaders. The reestablishment of the Yeshiva in New York signaled the beginning of a new life for the students who had upheld the banner of Jewish learning during the Holocaust years, first in Poland and Lithuania and then in Japan and China. Inspired and encouraged by their spiritual mentors, those young men had managed to overcome war, hunger, and all manner of physical and spiritual threats to their lives. As they adjusted to a new life of peace and security in the United States, many of these scholars threw themselves into the task of rebuilding existing American Torah centers and founding new institutions of higher Jewish learning. As leaders, instructors, organizers, and specialists on the highest levels of Torah study, they led a worldwide effort to reconstruct Torah life in the Free World.

The miraculous rescue of the Mirrer Yeshiva, together with remnants of other yeshivos, proved to be a Divine vehicle for transplanting the eternal Torah to a new continent and to open the new era of post-Holocaust rebirth.

The Religious Faith of Polish Jewry

September 1, 1939 began like any autumn morning in Warsaw, the bustling capital of Poland. A new school year was about to begin, and children on the way to their classes would have mingled with crowds of workers and businessmen hurrying to factories and stores. It would have been the typical beginning of a working day in the metropolis of Warsaw. But only all too early, dozens of warplanes appeared suddenly in the clear blue skies over Warsaw. People looked up in surprise, but also with pride, because they had never before seen so impressive a display of what they took to be their own air force. Although they knew that mighty German armies had been massing at the borders of their country, it did not occur to any of them that the warplanes overhead might not be their own.

Within minutes, tens, then hundreds of tiny objects appeared high in the sky, looking in the distance like little candies showering over the heads of the people of Warsaw. They grew bigger and more ominous, reaching frightening dimensions as they fell onto the streets of the unsuspecting capital. In those last seconds before the bombs hit their targets, the people realized, too late, the scope of the approaching tragedy. Death and destruction rained down on the capital of Poland. Between crashing walls and from inside collapsing houses, screams of agony and pain filled the air; people in panic stumbled toward shelters amidst overturned streetcars, over rubble and debris.

Germany had attacked! Poland, unprepared for war, was butchered without there even having been a declaration of war, while the world stood by in shocked disbelief. Thus was World War II thrust upon mankind.

People throughout Poland, particularly terror-stricken Jews, huddled around the few available radios, following the reports of the latest developments with increasing despair, realizing the devastating defeat that the Polish army was suffering under the mighty blows of the German war machine. The Germans had invaded Poland from three different directions. The round-the-clock bombings of the German Luftwaffe had brought all transportation and movements of the Polish army to a standstill.

World War II had burst upon Poland with an incredible onslaught of German firepower and a force that stunned the world in its ferocity and speed. The swift and crushing defeat of Poland was the world's first view of the modern concept of blitzkrieg. Cut off from all supplies under the crippling effect of the blitzkrieg warfare, Poland had no choice but to negotiate for surrender.

After three weeks of war, Poland ceased to exist as an independent nation. The western part of the country was overrun by the victorious German hordes, while its eastern sector was soon occupied by Red armies that poured into its territory from the east. The armies of the two occupying powers met at the agreed upon dividing line, the Bug River, and occupied simultaneously all of Poland, including its once flourishing centers of Jewish life.

Following the total disruption of Jewish religious life in Russia after the Bolshevik Revolution of 1917, Poland had become the spiritual focus for Jews the world over. In the period between the two world wars, Poland was the greatest center of Jewish thought and scholarship to which Jews throughout the world looked as the guarantee of Jewish survival.

In 1939 the Germans went to war against the civilized world in general and against the Jewish people in particular. Their attack against the Jews took the form of a crusade unprecedented in world history. Wherever the German armies appeared, the destruction of the Jewish population followed in short order.

But even in those dark days in the fall of 1939, the Jews of Poland gave a shining account of their spiritual qualities.

After two weeks of warfare, most of Poland's territory had been overrun; only Warsaw was still holding out in hopeless resistance. In a final, futile burst of patriotism, the defenders of the Polish capital desperately attempted to continue the war they knew was lost. Meanwhile, Warsaw's Jewish population had swelled to several times its original number, because all the Jewish refugees from the countryside, in a hopeless attempt to escape the advancing enemy, had flocked to Warsaw as a last refuge.

Heavy German artillery pounded the encircled city from all sides with cruel precision. The heavy guns were aimed especially at the civilian population of Warsaw's Jewish neighborhoods. At the same time, German planes flew unhindered at rooftop height, releasing their bombs, with the Jewish homes of Warsaw as their prime targets. Huddled in the shelters and cellars of Nalevki, Tvarda, and Grzybovska Streets, those who survived felt each earthshaking explosion as if the bomb had hit the house next door — even when, in fact, the planes had dropped their deadly loads a mile or two away.

Finally, the Polish commander realized that he had no choice but to surrender and end his suicidal resistance.

The cease-fire was set for noontime on Wednesday, September 27, 1939, the eve of the *Sukkos* holiday. The Germans were punctual in holding their fire, and the ear-shattering noise of exploding bombs stopped abruptly. The sudden silence was a strange contrast to the days and weeks of uninterrupted shelling from the ground and bombing from the air.

Among those Jewish refugees caught in the siege of Warsaw was Rabbi Yitzchok Ze'ev Soloveitchik, the venerable rabbi of the city of Brest-Litovsk (Brisk). He had been vacationing in the summer resort of Otvotsk, a suburb of Warsaw, and was among the hundreds of thousands who had fled to the capital when war broke out. Years later he still spoke of his impressions of the first night following the cease-fire in Warsaw.

As the armistice went into effect, people began to dig themselves out of their shelters. Hundreds of Warsaw's Jewish survivors leaped from the cellars and rubble, grabbed broken doors and window frames, and pulled them together for the construction of *sukkos*. By the arrival of sunset — 5:40 P.M. of that day — numerous *sukkos* greeted the holiday of the Tabernacles (even though others had been destroyed by roving bands of German soldiers and their Polish helpers).

What a perplexing phenomenon of Jewish faith revealed itself in these moments of Jewish suffering! There was barely a person among those who came forth from the ruins and shelters who had not lost close family during the continual, two-week bombardment that preceded the surrender. Who, in those moments, was in full control of himself after paralyzing weeks of constant fear and terror, with inadequate sleep and food?

"How could anyone think, in those moments, of any *mitzvos*?" admiringly asked the venerable Rabbi of Brisk, popularly called "*Reb* Velvele." "How can I compare myself at all to these ordinary Jews who were such great men of faith, to those Jews of Warsaw!"

How could anyone explain those speedily constructed *sukkos* in the midst of all the hardship and suffering? Those tailors and shoemakers, craftsmen and shopkeepers of Jewish Warsaw, who had suffered and lost their loved ones and the fruits of their lifelong toil and who faced a future fraught with almost unthinkable dangers, still had sufficient strength to focus their minds on the problem of fulfilling the *mitzvos* connected with the approaching Sukkos festival — building a *sukka* and obtaining a *lulov* and an *esrog*. There is only one explanation. The observance of *mitzvos* was the lifeblood of these Jews of Warsaw, and it was therefore the focus of all their thoughts, even in the midst of unspeakable suffering and terror.

Night fell upon Warsaw, the first night under the German occupation. A dawn-to-dusk curfew had been announced so that no one was in the street except the soldiers of the conqueror.

The Mitzva of the Esrog

The rear of the house that the Rabbi of Brisk shared with another Jewish survivor had been destroyed in the bombardment. The rabbi's roommate sat on the ground in stunned silence. In those fateful days, who was not despondent over the losses in his life? Who was not heartbroken when everything one had lived for had vanished in a matter of a few weeks? The Rabbi of Brisk attempted to comfort him.

"*Reb Yid*," he said, "don't give in to mournful thoughts. Remember it is *yom tov* now. Our holiday of Sukkos has begun within a *tzoras rabbim*, when a Jewish community is in dire distress with the losses we all have suffered. But if we share our common grief perhaps we will find the strength to rise above our personal losses."

"*Rebbe*," the man replied with some agitation, "that is not what upsets me. What is worrying me is how I will be able to fulfill the *mitzva* of reciting a blessing over an *esrog* this year — tomorrow morning!"

"If that's what depresses you, my dear friend," the rabbi comforted him, "I have help for you! I have an *esrog* right here with me."

"Really, Rebbe? Can it be true?" A complete change came over this man. He leaped to his feet with new life.

The Mitzva of the Esrog

The cloud that had darkened the face of this survivor of Warsaw's bombardment disappeared in a matter of seconds.

At last, he succumbed to his exhaustion, and the blessing of sleep fell upon him. Before long, Reb Velvele too fell asleep.

It was still dark when the Rabbi of Brisk was awakened by the noise of a crowd. He cautiously stepped to the door of his gutted chamber. To his amazement, he faced the front of a long line of Jews stretching for several blocks. Turning to his roommate for an explanation, he heard the story of the Warsaw Jews' religious faith and devotion.

"This year," explained his roommate, "there are only four sets of *lulovim* and *esrogim* in all of Warsaw, because the Germans bombed all of the trains and moving stock before Rosh Hashana, and no *esrogim* could reach the capital. The other three *esrogim* were secured, like yours, far in advance through the special effort of alert observers of the *mitzva*. These other three were the only *esrogim* available to this large community of Jews, swelled to many times its original size by the endless influx of refugees. When you comforted me by revealing your valuable possession of an *esrog*, I passed the word along and soon the news spread all over Warsaw of another *esrog* in town. These people have been waiting in line since last evening. They have stood all night long in this endless column for the *mitzva* of holding your *esrog*, braving the German curfew and overcoming their own despair.

"I know one cannot give preferential treatment to anyone. Everyone must wait his turn to perform the *mitzva*. But there is one older man I know who came here from the suburb of Praga. His turn won't come until the late afternoon. Could preference perhaps be given to him as an exceptional case? He has to be home in time for *yom tov sheini*, the second day of Sukkos, in order for him to bury a close member of his family."

The rabbi concurred and added, "These Jews, displaying so much self-denial for a *mitzva*, should be allowed to perform it before me! How can I compare myself to these wonderful Jews in their quest for *mitzvos*?"

As dawn approached, the sound of sirens was suddenly heard. Truckloads of German troopers drove up. The soldiers jumped off the trucks and attacked the line of Jews with their wooden rifle butts, clubbing mercilessly left and right and shouting with murderous anger, "Don't you Jews know that we proclaimed a curfew! We smashed your Polish armies; how dare you defy us!" The screams of the many beaten civilians and the moans of the injured, who lay on the ground, filled the air. Having dispersed the long line, the Germans hurried on to other places.

Five minutes later, the same line had formed again, waiting in anxious yearning for daybreak, the time to begin performing the precious *mitzva* of *esrog* and *lulov*.

Poland's Torah Centers Begin to Move

The tragedy of Polish Jewry had also engulfed its Torah centers, the yeshivos. The great talmudical academies of Mir, Kamenitz, Kletsk, Lublin, Lubavitch, Grodno, Novardok, Baranovitch, Pinsk, as well as other lesser known yeshivos of distinction were all directly in the path of the Heavenly judgment that fell upon Poland's Jewry. Minds became occupied with thoughts of how and where to escape. Among the outstanding Torah centers where an intensive level of Torah study was maintained in the face of all adversity, was the Yeshiva of Mir. It was now part of the Soviet occupation zone.

One night early in October, 1939, a student of the Mirrer Yeshiva listened to a clandestine radio broadcast report from Radio London, beamed at occupied Europe. He heard a report that Vilna, in northern Poland, which had been occupied by the Soviet army, would be ceded to neighboring neutral Lithuania. The implication was electrifying. Perhaps this was the way to a miraculous escape from captivity! Whoever would be in Vilna when it was taken over by Lithuania would automatically be saved from the dangers and suffering of subjugation and would be able to enjoy freedom once more and a life in the Free World.

Now with this broadcast, an unprecedented mood seemed to pervade the Mir Yeshiva community and to exert a powerful grip on everyone's mind. It was as if an overpowering Heavenly inspiration was galvanizing the entire Yeshiva into action. Within forty-eight hours the rabbinical college was on the move. Without any planning or specific directives, hundreds of students, each independently and on his own initiative, packed his belongings and scrambled to get a horse and wagon or any other possible means of transport to reach the nearest railroad station, Horodzei. From there they traveled by train to their goal — the city of Vilna.

What was the basis for this mass emigration? Certainly there was nothing factual or confirmed, nothing but a rumor overheard on the radio!

Nevertheless, forty-eight hours later, the yeshiva town of Mir seemed very much deserted, because an almost total exodus of its yeshiva students had taken place. Even many years later, no one could explain the sudden spell that the rumor about Vilna cast upon the students of Mir, propelling them into action despite an abundance of doubts. It seemed as if a Heavenly power had guided everyone's thoughts to a single course of action.

In the end, a sizable part of the students of most Polish yeshivos and almost the entire Mirrer Yeshiva turned up in Vilna. There they lived under the most trying conditions, including a lack of housing and food, until Vilna's final reentry into the Free World on October 28, 1939, became reality.

For a brief period, a large part of the Yeshiva population, the guarantors of Torah for the Jewish people, was safe and resumed its studies in the city of Vilna and in other parts of tiny but free Lithuania.

Profile of a Miracle

What was the strange twist in history that allowed Vilna to become the center for the miraculous rescue of the yeshivos of Poland?

Rabbi Yechezkel Levenstein, the famous exponent of Jewish thought in Mirrer Yeshiva, analyzed the pivotal historical events that set the stage for this dramatic rescue. "Divine Providence," he said, "wanted to save Torah and its scholars from destruction. That is why, in His wondrous ways, God started to spin, almost twenty years before, assorted threads of history, which He eventually wove into a unique tapestry for survival."

On October 9, 1920, after the two friendly, neighboring countries of Lithuania and Poland had established a mutually recognized border, the strange incident of a one-man war wrecked the peaceful relations of these good neighbors and left them shattered for the next twenty years.

Without the consent of his own government — so it was officially stated — a Polish general, Lucian Zeligowski, marched with a private army into Vilna, which was then the capital of Lithuania, in order to annex it to Poland in his own name. This act of piracy created a furor in the League of Nations in Geneva — the United Nations of those days — that did not subside for many years. The Polish government officially disavowed the action of its general as irresponsible and mutinous.

However, three years later the city of Vilna was incorporated into the Republic of Poland. Lithuania severed all diplomatic relations with Poland, and a state of no-relations between the two countries continued for the next two decades till Poland's collapse at the outbreak of World War II.

The strange episode of Vilna, its annexation and integration into the Polish Republic, and the sudden reversal of its fortunes — with its return to the country of Lithuania — were the first steps in a chain of events, designed by Providence to lift the community of Torah leaders and its students out of the encirclement of death and destruction and to lead them forward to freedom and security.

For the Torah camp, the "Vilna Miracle" had other and more far-reaching implications, discovered only after the war when the German archives were forcibly opened. In *Ness Hatzalah*, E.J. Hertzman writes of the nonaggression pact between Hitler's Reich and the Soviet Union, struck shortly before the outbreak of World War II.* This world-shaking von Ribbentrop-Molotov agreement at once united two deadly enemies — Fascism and Communism — and by securing Germany's vast frontiers in the East, it unleashed Hitler's armies to overrun the Western World, destroy countries and enslave nations.

The most startling phenomenon of this pact was that the same brutal powers, bent on the destruction of nations without regard for any human rights, should so uncharac-

---

*Rabbi E.J. Hertzman and Rabbi C.U. Lipschitz, *Escape to Shanghai*: (New York: Bais Veyelepole, 1981), 1.

teristically consider the legitimate right of tiny Lithuania to her capital, Vilna! The German archives revealed that the return of Vilna to Lithuania, among other delineations of future borderlines in Eastern Europe, was agreed upon in a special, secret appendix to the nonaggression pact.

Thus the infamous von Ribbentrop-Molotov pact, which became the foundation for world destruction and maniacal persecution of Jews, turned into a key tool for the rescue of yeshivos and Torah scholars, the soul of the Jewish people.

Only twenty years later were seemingly unrelated events recognized and identified in great awe and amazement as the necessary preconditions that led to the rescue of the yeshivos and their Torah scholars, who would become the leaders and guarantors of the future of Jewry. Torah sages then identified unusual events that Providence brought about for the construction of this ark of rescue named Vilna. In 1938, just a year before the outbreak of World War II, Poland held a strange mobilization of its military forces against tiny Lithuania. A unique and bizarre "war for peaceful relations" was Poland's declared intention. Its ultimatum called for true neighborliness to replace a peace of no-relations that existed between the two neighbors.

The basic conditions were: Establishing full diplomatic relations, rebuilding the railroad line between Kovno and Vilna, and restoring commerce, communications and highways across the border to their respective interior areas.

These conditions paved the way for the deliverance of the Torah camp in the oncoming storm.

All the rescue efforts for further escape that were enabled by the transfer of Vilna to the Republic of Lithuania seemed condemned to futility because the refugees lacked the most basic tool — a passport. There was no way to obtain it at a time when their country, Poland, did not exist anymore.

Furthermore, the desperate hunt for visas at consulates required means of transportation and easy access from Vilna to Kovno that did not exist during the break-off of all communication between Poland and Lithuania.

However, as late as 1938, at the approach of World War II, tiny Lithuania complied with and fulfilled, within six months, all the conditions of its mighty neighbor. Diplomatic relations were restored and a Polish consulate in Kovno was established.

When Poland, at the end of 1939, was only a government-in-exile in London, it still was able to transfer the previously established Polish consulate in Kovno to a "Polish desk" in the British consulate. Thus the Polish representative could issue legal travel documents to his desperate Polish refugees in Lithuania. These travel documents, called Polish passports, became the lifesaving device for obtaining transit and exit visas.

Also, the hunt for visas was now made possible by the railroad and other frequent means of transportation from Vilna to Kovno.

The venerable rabbi of Brisk made this unusual event of 1938 one of his favorite observations, "Now we understand why the highway and the railroad line were constructed so quickly."

Lithuanian Jews — Embodiment of Torah and Chessed

Even though their life was still a paradise compared to the sufferings of their loved ones who had stayed behind in occupied Poland, the transplanted Torah scholars in Vilna tasted the bitterness of life as uprooted refugees. The Lithuanian Jews rose to the occasion with all the strength and compassion at their command, extending the proverbial Lithuanian Jewish hospitality to the refugees from Poland. Although they themselves had lost most of their properties and their means of livelihood due to the Soviet occupation of Lithuania in June 1940, they often shared the very last of their supplies with their unfortunate brethren, the refugees from neighboring, devastated Poland. This generosity took place under circumstances and conditions so trying, that if not personally witnessed and experienced, one could never have imagined them. No host and their hospitality were ever tested as severely under the most trying of circumstances as these Lithuanian Jews. Propelled by superlative Jewish principles and motives, they performed unparalleled deeds of generosity and hospitality for their Polish brethren.

Kaisiadoris, the one-time border station of the Vilna-Kovno (Lithuania) railroad line that brought the refugees from Poland and Vilna into the Lithuanian "heartland," was for many refugees a gateway to the Free World in tiny Lithuania. A train packed with refugees would sometimes wait on the tracks of this former Polish-Lithuanian border town for hours, even now, after the incorporation of Vilna and its environs into Lithunia.

Suddenly, a Jew from town approached the train, shouting desperately, "Help! Help! Jewish brothers, please, help, please!"

People stuck their heads out of the train's windows; some even got out of the train in apprehension. "What's the matter, what happened?"

The man replied, "I live just opposite the station, on the other side of the Station Square."

More intensive questions followed from the passengers of the train. "So tell us, why are you so upset?"

The man went on, "Please, good people, come along! Right opposite the station, there, that is my house, come over to my house, I beg of you. You have another thirty minutes before the train leaves! Come quickly!"

Two, three, five and more refugees followed the man out of curiosity and compassion. "Reb Yid, what's the matter in your house?" someone inquired. "Is somebody sick there? Tell us, please, what happened?"

"Oh no! Nothing of the kind, thank God," the man answered. "But you still must come and help us. We prepared the best things that we could offer you people. You must come in for a short while," he insisted, "to have a bite and rest. Please, don't turn us down…" This man's "problem" was typical of the average Lithuanian Jew.

The poor refugees were treated to a hot meal by people who themselves were only of average means, and that only when measured by the very modest standards prevailing then in Eastern Europe. A sumptuous table was set, and the host, his wife, and his family invited their guests to sit down and eat so that they might strengthen themselves for the next stage of the journey into an unknown future. The desire of this Jew and his family to share, to support and to cheer up these unfortunate brethren they had never seen before was so irresistibly powerful that they virtually begged these strangers to take advantage of their hospitality. Their burning desire was to help and, consequently, to see the refugees strengthened and relieved on their path of hardship. The refugees did not have to search for synagogues and schools to get food, shelter, and housing. Their fellow Jews willingly shared their modest homes and their food; they even gave up their own beds, sleeping on the floor or on makeshift beds made of boards, so that their guests might be comfortable. Five, even ten guests might be welcomed into a poor three-room apartment; and the more guests, the happier the host, because the greater would be his satisfaction at being able to fulfill the *mitzva* of hospitality and of helping to bring relief to fellow Jews in distress.

In Slobodka, a suburb of Lithuania's capital, Kovno, the Communists had confiscated a bakery, which had been built up through a lifetime of hard work. They permitted the baker to continue working in his former shop, but only as an employee and only for a short transition period until new workers and apprentices could be trained to take over. Even his official savings had been expropriated by the local *soviet* (workers' council). What a bleak future this baker had to look forward to!

Yet this man's faith in God and the depth of his Jewish commitment kept him strong and enabled him to overcome all adversities. He continued to provide a shining example in the practice of Torah and *mitzvos* as before, when his house had been known for its exceptional hospitality. Every Sabbath morning after services he continued to invite guests to his home — not just one or two people, but as many as he could persuade to join him for the Sabbath meal. He performed this act of generosity even on weekdays, prodding refugees at random to come to his house "for just a plate of hot soup." He kept oversized kettles with food simmering on his stove. An army kettle filled with rich, hearty soup was the main "equipment" of this extraordinary hospitality. His guests assumed that such mass feedings had the support of a Jewish relief organization or some local charity fund, and they were startled when they learned subsequently that their host had used his meager financial reserves to feed the refugees, notwithstanding his family's own desperate plight in those days. Everyone in the baker's family busily served the guests, even the children, in spite of their membership in the Komsomol (Communist Youth League). "Don't worry about us, we have enough," was their usual response to all questions regarding their own financial resources.

The situation was bleak for all of Lithuania's Jews. Their system of life had been shattered by the new Communist order after the annexation in the summer of 1940. Still, many Jews like the baker and his family remained undaunted. Their unique Jewish approach to life and its problems comforted them and gave them the moral strength to assure themselves that these refugees were in greater distress and much less fortunate than they themselves, and therefore in greater need of help than they, the "native Lithuanians," who at least still had a roof over their heads. Countless instances of such great selflessness and absolute devotion to humanity were encountered all over Lithuania, even in the most remote Jewish settlements.

The following case of the wealthiest man and leader of a *shtetl*—starting in the months before the annexation—was witnessed by this writer. This wealthy man's wife had quite a number of servants and maids in the house as well as hands in the fields. But the lady of the house insisted on doing all of the cooking, baking, and serving when it came to helping her refugee guests. "Aren't they Torah scholars, yeshiva men? Haven't they all lost their homes and families in Poland? I would not let anyone deprive me of the privilege to give room and board to such people!" And so she personally involved herself in all phases of hospitality — preparing delicious, home-baked bread and all kinds of fancy pastries, using her best resources: flour from their own mill, fresh vegetables from the family's own farm and fruits from the garden, served with fresh milk — chocolate flavored — from the family's own cows. All these delicacies were served on exquisite china, personally, by the rich lady of the house. Such elaborate breakfasts awaited her guests upon their return from the morning services. The refugees were treated to all the luxuries of her home, where they were treated more like the spoiled children of the rich hosts than as merely distinguished guests of the house.

Trapped Again

Thousands of Torah leaders, *roshey yeshiva*, yeshiva students and other Jewish refugees from Poland were trapped again in June 1940, when the Red Army suddenly occupied the still independent and neutral Baltic states, Lithuania, Latvia and Estonia. In time, the Jewish refugees from Poland would be considered "recaptured criminals"! Not only were they clergymen, one of the most dangerous labels in the Soviet Union that designated a citizen as one of the worst enemies of the people and of the Communist regime, but they also carried the stigma of actually having tried once to escape from Communism by fleeing into Lithuania from the Russian sector of occupied Poland. More than once, their brothers and benefactors, the native Lithuanian Jews, asked them with deep concern, "To where will you now escape? Unfortunately this is a final trap from which there is no way out."

Actually, there was no more hopeless situation than the fate of a Torah student in Russia, because "No Work — No Bread" was the party slogan for the enslaved masses of Russia. While there was not much more in store than that "piece of bread" for a large part of Russia's population under the rule of Stalin, it still spelled survival for the impoverished average individual. But the price for this magic piece of bread was exorbitant! It was the full exploitation of the individual and his energies for the machine of the Communist state in which the individual citizen is but a mindless cog. Yet, as "enemies" of the regime, these yeshiva students were unable to even obtain the permit for work, and consequently could not even look forward to the "privilege" of securing work and bread.

Furthermore, if the "clericals" had been able to obtain work papers, their problems would not have come to an end. The work week under the Communist system at the time was five days, but this did not mean that the workers enjoyed America's two-day weekend of freedom to do as they pleased. Five days of work were followed by only one day of "rest" *and* political indoctrination, followed by another five days of work. This system was designed to keep adherents of organized religions — Jews, Christians and Moslems alike — from observing the days of rest and the holidays hallowed by their respective faiths. It was all part of the Communist plan to eradicate religion. One week the five-day cycle might end on a Monday, the next week on a Sunday, then on a Saturday, and next on Friday, the Sabbath of the Moslems. Thus the sixth day, the "day of rest," would never be on a specific day of the week, in order to prevent establishing a definite day-of-rest pattern. If one were absent from work on the Sabbath of one's own religion — when that day did not coincide with the end of that particular five-day cycle — it meant that one would automatically lose his position and thus be left without a means of livelihood. As a result, observant Jews who refused to give up their Saturday Sabbath could not obtain employment. How then, could they hope to survive in Russia or marry and establish families of their own? What Jewish girl would tie her life to the fate of any individual considered an outcast in Soviet society, presaging the bleakest of all existences? The yeshivos and their students seemed to be doomed; their future wrapped in hopelessness and fraught with danger, destined to perish in the slave labor camps of Siberia.

The yeshiva students, from the Torah point of view, were always the elite of their people, the future of their nation, the standard-bearers of Jewish thought and survival. They were now caught in a trap, destined for destruction between the paws of the Russian bear. They faced their problems with unbelievable strength and undaunted faith. When they were asked "Where will you go now?" the reply would come forth again and again with unshaken certainty: "The Almighty has performed miracles for us in the past, and so Divine Providence will save us again from the Communist trap all around us."

They were able to give these answers in perfect faith because they had inculcated in themselves the realities of Torah, the eternal values of life.

The Soviet Deportation Trap

The first victims trapped in the snare of Communist trickery were an estimated two hundred thousand Jews from Russian-occupied Poland.

Shortly after the Red Army consolidated its grip on the eastern part of Poland, the Russians made an announcement aimed specifically at the Jewish population which was trapped there. After a specified deadline nobody would be permitted to leave Soviet-occupied territory. But until the incorporation of the eastern part of Poland into the Soviet Union was completed, those who desired to join relatives in countries like America or Palestine could apply for exit permits. What Jewish family did not have a member in America or Palestine or could not discover a relative if it meant escaping a life of misery under the Communists? Jews eagerly flocked to register for exit permits, and the Russians busily noted down the long lists of applicants.

Six weeks later, the army designated a certain night for air raid drills and curfew practice for the civilian population throughout the Soviet-occupied part of Poland. Special instructions for total blackout were posted to prepare everyone for eventual enemy attacks. That same night, throughout the blacked-out regions of Byelorussia

Operation: Torah Rescue

(White Russia) and Galicia, Russian secret police went from street to street and from house to house to arrest all the people whose names were on their lists of prospective emigrants. Those lists had been turned into a blacklist of self-confessed enemies of the Communist regime. Some two hundred thousand unsuspecting Jews were dragged from their beds, given a few minutes to gather a few personal belongings, and then escorted by armed guards to waiting trains that took them as political prisoners into the icy wastelands of Siberia.

The lamentations and tears of the people who were completely unprepared for this sudden calamity were indescribable. Allowed to take with them only a few belongings, these Jews found themselves completely unprotected against the harsh climate of Siberia. Exposed to icy storms and temperatures of fifty-five degrees Fahrenheit below zero, they died by the thousands in Siberia's forests and steppes. It was almost miraculous that as many as sixty percent of the exiled survived in spite of the complete unpreparedness of their bodies and minds for these ordeals. Often, husbands and wives were separated, brides and grooms were torn apart to suffer in slave labor camps thousands of miles apart; thus even the human comfort and consolation of their loved ones were denied these exiles.

At the time of these tragedies, it was impossible to imagine that just half a year later these most miserable and unfortunate victims would be considered the "fortunate ones" who were envied by their fellow Jews when the German hordes invaded Russia. The abducted two hundred thousand Jews were eventually the lucky ones who were spared the infamous German death camps, which were established in the captured Polish territories. Thus did Divine Providence turn the victims of one of the most tragic events into objects of envy!

The Greatest Folly

Barely six weeks after the great tragedy that befell the deported Polish-Byelorussian and West Galician Jews, a renewed momentum of thoughts once more gripped the minds of the Torah youth and swayed them — this time into applying for Russian exit visas. None of the observers could assess whether the new decisions taken were the result of new developments or simply steps taken in a mood of despair and hopelessness after finding themselves once again completely trapped by the Communists.

At first it was just a trickle, a few individuals pioneering the spontaneous action. Suddenly more and more refugees joined in a snowballing movement that enveloped an increasing number of yeshiva groups. They beleaguered the Russian Commissariat with applications for the "impossible": a permit to leave Russia! Such a demand for exit visas from the Soviet Union was taboo; it was considered a forbidden and even criminal act, a plot against the regime! How then could an entire group of scholars, men of understanding, embark on such a suicidal undertaking? This was especially remarkable after the drastic warning that had just been delivered in the form of the tragic fate of the forced mass transports of Jews to

Siberia for their sole "crime" of having applied for emigration visas and their implied rejection of the Communist regime.

Many of the yeshiva applicants were showered with letters from family and friends in Russian-occupied Poland, pleading with them not to undertake the dangerous steps they were planning. Merely expressing the idea of leaving the Soviet "paradise" could bring untold suffering upon the individual and upon his entire community.

No responsible analysis of the situation could refute the reasoning behind all those warnings. The known facts led to only one clear-cut, reasonable conclusion: to desist from the dangerous course of applying for exit visas.

Once again, however, the thinking and sentiments of individuals and, ultimately, groups were gripped by an unprecedented force that propelled the Torah youth* along their risky path with undiminished fervor.

In those fateful days, a member of the yeshiva group decided to solve this dilemma by invoking the power of the famous *gorol*, "the lot" of the Vilna Gaon. The *gorol* is cast with a one-volume Bible. It provides desperately needed advice in critical situations and solutions to vital problems of either individuals or an entire community. It guides the

---

* The student leaders, the brains propelling the rescue actions, were the top Torah minds among them, men with a deep sense of moral responsibility, who became the Torah leaders of the generation after the Holocaust. Untiring deliberations and painstaking planning of minute details preceded every action and its detailed execution. Their history-making efforts were complemented by the endeavors of dedicated helpers and agents, the selfless servants of the community.

Regarding their names, one should state that the intent of this work is not to be a reporter's chronicle or to accord the personal credit due to personalities involved in this historic rescue effort.

Rabbi Eliezer Yehuda Finkel, Mirrer Rosh Yeshiva

inquirer to the Biblical verse that is considered the Providential response to the dilemma, the solution to the individual's or group's problem. The solution, though, may need interpretation by a qualified scholar.

The "answer" which the inquiring scholar received was given in Exodus 19:4, which reads, "And I will carry you on eagles' wings and I will deliver you to Me." What clearer and more outspoken answer could one want for all the basic doubts about the risks of this undertaking than the words of this Biblical announcement?

Of course, turning to the Vilna Gaon's *gorol* is tied to a number of conditions, not the least of which concerns the person casting it. In this instance, it was handled by a noted scholar among this group.

The NKVD Under Siege

All day and till late at night, desperate refugees stood in the true style of a Russian *kolayka* (waiting line), winding all around the building and along the hallways and stairs of the *NKVD* in Vilna, the Office of the National Commissariat for Internal Affairs, the Communist Secret Police, in order to obtain exit visas.

At 2 A.M. the offices were still busy turning out exit visas, an unprecedented experience in Russia, when for years they had accorded these priceless documents to only a few privileged individuals. Now, however, the Russian secret police were virtually besieged by the "enemies of the state"! More than once, the Russian *commissar* threatened "to have all you bourgeois parasites shot against the same wall where you are lined up at this very moment." Mountains of paper rubles were piled up on the desks and tables of the commissar's room, the accumulated fees charged for these invaluable documents, merely named exit visas but actually delivering a lifesaving device to its owners. The issuing of all these exit permits was an unheard of phenomenon in the annals of the regime. "Don't you wolves have pity on me?" exclaimed the Vilna NKVD head, Comrade Schlossberg. "And on all those tired comrades who work at this late hour past midnight — for bloodsuckers and parasites!"

This development was an unbelievable change of the fundamental Soviet policy that had consistently erected an iron wall around its citizenry. Nobody had been allowed to leave the Russian "paradise," in order to keep the world from discovering the misery of Soviet life. It therefore became a basic tenet of Soviet policy and its internal propaganda to consider the desire to leave the Communist homeland tantamount to treason. What had brought this puzzling turnabout in so fundamental a Russian principle?

According to a leak from government circles in the newly established Soviet Lithuanian People's Republic, the puppet Communist government had made the disposition of the refugees a cardinal point of national pride and reputation. Lithuanian hospitality for the masses of refugees from defeated Poland — so it was argued to the Russian overlords — had gained for the nation an illustrious reputation on the stage of world opinion. The millions of dollars fed into the Lithuanian economy by donations from abroad, as subsidies to support the Jewish refugees, had significantly strengthened the treasury of the government. Lithuanian pride and dignity therefore demanded that the refugees not be dumped into the wilderness of Siberia. Such an act would make a mockery of all the exemplary conduct of the tiny nation that had been guided by lofty humanitarian motives.

Reports from reliable sources said that the Soviet bosses had been impressed by the strange insistence of their new satellite and had given in to the demand for the release of the refugees.

As this unheard of demand was granted, some two thousand refugees, most from a very religious background, finally surged through the breach in the "iron wall." They were looked at by people all over Russia as if they were men from another planet, so remote was the possibility of even a single individual ever being allowed to leave the Soviet Union.

To appreciate the extent of this miraculous phenomenon, one must again recall the facts of life in Communist Russia, where only a few people had managed to leave — under most unusual circumstances. For example, Rabbi Kalmanowitz had managed to obtain permission for his father to leave Russia by engaging the services of M. Litvinow, the Soviet foreign secretary, during the latter's historic visit to America, through intercession by a U.S. Senator with pro-Russian leanings.

Another example of such an unusual escape from Russia was that of the late Rebbe of Lubavitch, Rabbi Yosef Y. Schneerson. After being sentenced to a long prison term for conducting religious activities among Jews, he was eventually released, owing to a singular combination of circumstances.

In the years following the Bolshevik Revolution, Russia was completely isolated from, and boycotted by, the outside world. The first attempt to pierce this isolation was a commercial treaty with the tiny neighboring country of Latvia. A member of the Latvian parliamentary delegation which negotiated this treaty, Mordechai Dubin, himself a follower of the Lubavitcher Rebbe, managed to obtain the release of the Jewish leader as one of the Russian concessions for this first treaty of commerce between Russia and another country. Thus, the treaty that was of special importance for the Soviet Union simultaneously enabled the Rebbe to leave Russia.

No wonder that these refugee-travelers were met with such incredulity and amazement when they divulged the facts of their mass exodus to people they met on their trek through the Russian part of the Euro-Asian continent.

The Advice of Torah

In the crucial years before World War II, even more than in tranquil times, the advice and counsel of giants of Torah, the Torah leaders of that generation, was sought in countless cases of individual distress and communal problems. In the wake of ever-worsening anti-Semitism in Eastern Europe, an especially burdensome question for individuals, groups and whole communities was more and more often posed: Should we emigrate?

The following situation typifies the quandaries faced by Jews during the Holocaust years. And the ruling handed down by the sage who was asked to resolve the quandary also explains away puzzlement about the lack of sufficient counsel during the events of this era.

When Germany and Russia carved up Poland, the dividing line between their armies became the river Bug, which also passed the nearby city of Brisk (Brest-Litovsk).

Masses of Jewish refugees fleeing the Germans approached the river Bug to cross to the Russian side of occupied Poland. Simultaneously, multitudes of other refugees fleeing Soviet occupation were making their way to the opposite bank. In their misery and desperation, the first group looked upon the second in wonder: How could any person in his right mind try to escape to the Germans? The other group thought just the opposite, since they were risking everything to escape from the Russians.

This dilemma demanded a solution! It was decided to seek a rabbinical response to the *shaileh* of where to run from a recognized judge in the Torah court of the city of Brisk.

The city's rabbinical court was headed at that time by the famous Rabbi Simcha Zelig Ryger, the supreme rabbinical judge of the Brisk community court. After listening to the stories of fear and terror from both sides, Reb Simcha Zelig finally rendered his ruling, the gist of which was as follows: We have entered only the initial phase of a war which in its characteristics and features — especially to the extent of its unparalleled, subhuman bestialities against Jews — is a war beyond human comprehension. Since the developments of these events defy our understanding, concepts or rational analysis, one cannot make Torah pronouncements on such matters. There can be no Torah ruling (*pesak*) on a subject (*sugyah*) beyond the grasp of human comprehension. [Torah judgments are based solely on facts which are subject and accessible to human analysis, except in certain Divine revelations. – author]

Rabbi Simcha Zelig Ryger's judgment and analysis have been completely vindicated by the events that unfolded during the war. Events proved the best of logical advice tragically incorrect, while irrational decisions often resulted in inexplicable rescue.

Thus Rabbi Simcha Zelig Ryger's Torah counsel affords insight into the character of the events of a special era that is described by the Biblical term *hester ponim*, an era of planned Divine concealment, when the Creator deliberately conceals Himself and denies mortals even the mere understanding of the afflictions to which His nation is exposed. An additional part of this punishment consists of being bereft of His guidance in one's quandaries. [See details in Isaiah 29:14, with the commentary of Metzudas Dovid, which reveals this epoch to be different from any other since Jewish nationhood.]

Leaving Russia For — Nowhere

Against incredible odds and under improbable circumstances, the escape from Russia was nothing short of miraculous. The story of how a haven of refuge came into being demands telling.

Exit visas from the Soviet Union were issued only for a definite country of destination. In those dark years of German persecutions no such final haven for homeless Jewish wanderers was available. While the Jewish populations of countries under German control were destined for annihilation, only a few lands opened their gates to Jewish families in severely limited numbers, or to children only. These were years of fear and persecution, and the quest for a place on the globe to which to escape was filled with heartbreak and desperation.

Asking for a Russian exit visa entailed the grave risk of deportation to Siberia. To apply for an exit visa without showing a place of destination was tantamount to performing a senseless act of self-destruction. What country would now open its gates to thousands of new Jewish refugees? Certainly there was no more unlikely a candidate for such a refuge than Japan, Germany's Axis ally.

In the twenty-one years between World Wars I and II,

Japan and Lithuania had developed many common interests. They were both neighbors of gigantic Communist Russia, and both felt threatened by Communist expansion. In addition, they shared mutual commercial interests. Japan needed Lithuania's agricultural products, while Lithuania was in need of Japan's industrial output. Nevertheless, Japan had not seen fit to have a consular representative in Lithuania during all those twenty-one years.

That may have been a serious omission in Japan's foreign policy. But what followed bordered on the incomprehensible! During 1940, approximately at the time of the annexation of Lithuania by the Russian army, the Imperial Japanese government went ahead with a decision that puzzled the world. At the very moment that Lithuania ceased to exist as an independent state — and England, France, and all the other major powers were about to close down their consulates and missions in Kovno, the capital of Lithuania — the Japanese government decided to open a consulate of its own in this occupied and abandoned country.

This strange decision was surpassed only by the action of the new Japanese consul, who added his own unique chapter to this tale. The new consul, Senpo Sugihara, on his own initiative, adopted a new policy reversing a long-established principle of his own government.

The years preceding World War II were desperate times for Jews attempting to escape their persecutors. Individually and in groups they attempted to flee Germany, and later, Middle and Eastern Europe, for their lives. But the gates of most of the world's countries were closed to them.

Japan was in the forefront of the many lands that had closed their doors to Jewish refugees. Not only did Japan deny refuge and rescue for even small groups of Jewish applicants, it also refused mere transit through Japan to another destination, lest an individual Jew become stranded on its territory. This closed-door policy to the victims of German persecution was extended by the Japanese to the point where they refused transit visas even through foreign territories that were merely under Japanese military control.

The city of Shanghai in China was a free city, an international port with free entry for travelers from all over the world. However, when the flow of refugees increased, Japan denied transit visas even through Japanese-occupied Manchuria, a vital link for traveling from Europe via the Trans-Siberian Railroad to Shanghai. With the Euro-Asian overland route blocked, Jewish refugees had to escape by using the more exhausting and costly sea route — all around Europe and Asia by way of the Suez Canal and the Indian Ocean to reach Shanghai.

In spite of these conditions, the recently arrived Japanese consul was approached by some refugees with a request — naive in terms of the political reality of Japanese policy — to approve Japanese transit visas for the trapped refugees. They hoped to use these Japanese visas for filling in the space marked "destination" on their applications for Russian exit visas! The Japanese consul at first explained that such transit visas were out of the question. But upon seeing the apparently endless column of refugees winding along the streets surrounding the consulate, he decided to supply such visas on his own responsibility. There was one provision the consul insisted upon: that each passport show the visa of a country of final destination to justify a mere "transit" visa through Japan. This simple stipulation, however, plunged the refugees back into the same dilemma they had faced regarding the Russian exit visa. In those dark, desperate days there just wasn't any country to which a Jew would be permitted to escape, especially from occupied Lithuania where the few remaining consulates were in the process of closing their doors.

One of the students of the Telshe Yeshiva, a Dutch subject, Nathan Gutwirt, hit upon the idea of approaching his own country's consul with a unique solution of a "final destination" visa. He suggested that the island of Curaçao, in the Dutch West Indies, be opened to receive the waves of Jewish refugees stranded in occupied Lithuania.

Much to the surprise of the yeshiva student, the Dutch consul revealed that admission to Curaçao did not require an entry visa. However, a landing permit had to be obtained from its governor. As electrifying as the Dutch consul's revelation was to the refugee community, it still did not satisfy the NKVD. The Russians insisted on an official permit entered on each passport to confirm this pronouncement of Dutch policy. After much foot-dragging, the Dutch consul finally agreed to stamp the refugees' passports with an official "permit" reading: "Entry into Curaçao does not require a visa."

As amazing as the actions of the Dutch consul is the story of Russia, a country letting no one out — but permitting these "clericals" to leave — and of Japan, barring Jews from merely passing through Japanese-occupied territories, but now granting two thousand refugees a stay even on the Japanese mainland. Equally startling is another link in this chain of incredible developments that was discovered years later by Dr. David Kranzler.* He interviewed the son of the Dutch consul in Kovno in 1939, J. Zwartendijk, who revealed that his father,

---

*Regarding all the details of this history-making endeavor, see Dr. David Kranzler, *Japanese, Nazis and Jews* (New York: Yeshiva University Press, 1976), 311-12. It gives an encyclopedic documentation of the Japanese national encounter with the Jewish people during the Holocaust years.

who had been the one to provide the famous Curaçao visas, had been just newly appointed as Dutch consul; his predecessor had been removed from his post when it was discovered that he was a Nazi sympathizer. The importance of such details at these crucial moments can hardly be overestimated.

The unbelievable had happened again. The designs, principles and policies of two great world powers had been set aside for the benefit and the rescue of a group of scholars, remnants of the European yeshiva community, who had dedicated their lives to the service of Torah ideals.

For Eastern European village people, leading quiet lives far removed from the world of commerce and politics, names like China, Japan or Curaçao were merely strange sounds out of a geography lesson. It attests to their desperation that these refugees chose to travel to such far-flung lands in their search for even a far-fetched solution.

The exciting news about the lifesaving Curaçao visas not only propelled people to the Dutch consulate but also created endless lines before the entrance to the Japanese consulate. The lines started to form long before the consulate office opened, often as early as midnight the night before.

What was even more perplexing in this strange episode was the personal attitude of the Japanese consul. Senpo Sugihara was warned that his issuing of these visas constituted insubordination since it directly contradicted his government's policy. Yet he continued his humanitarian activity undaunted, emphasizing that he could not refuse the appeals of hapless refugees attempting to escape the claws of the Russian bear. He instructed his staff to continue issuing the transit visas because "none of these people will ever be able to leave Russia anyway. No one ever did so in the past. So let them feel happier in their desperate situation."

When most of the refugees had had the lifesaving Japanese transit visas stamped into their passports and had taken the final step of submitting them for their Russian exit permits, orders arrived from the Japanese Foreign Office to immediately stop issuing any further transit visas. The consul was reprimanded for his unauthorized actions and soon afterwards the Japanese consulate in Kovno was closed. Sugihara was demoted and transferred to the Japanese consulates in Berlin and Bucharest.

In the episode of the Japanese visas, one cannot but be impressed by the sequence of unprecedented and seemingly irrational details, through which Divine Providence paved the escape route for His Torah elite. This deliverance took place against unbelievable odds despite the principles of governments and their long-established national policies. Even in the so-called minor details, one is taken aback by the extraordinary meshing of the pieces of this unique mosaic of occurrences that paved the way to the final survival and rescue.

What but Divine Providence could explain, for instance, the following facts: all contacts with the Japanese consul had to be channeled through his secretary, an ethnic German, Wolfgang Gutsche, who spoke fluent Lithuanian, Russian, English, and German and was an ardent follower of the Fuehrer. Some even maintain that Gutsche was planted in the consulate to spy for the German Secret Service. (After the closing of the Japanese consulate, Herr Gutsche was "repatriated" to Germany to join the ranks of the notorious German S.A. — storm troopers.)

Since Gutsche supplied Sugihara with the political background of all the matters on his agenda, he could easily have stopped the consul from granting the Jews the vital transit visas that would save them from the annihilation that was a cornerstone of the Third Reich policy. Nevertheless, this ardent follower of his Fuehrer confided to the yeshiva group's "diplomatic representative," Moshe Zupnick, that he would support the preposterous request for hundreds of Japanese visas because he had "once had an affair with a Jewish sweetheart and therefore disagreed with the Fuehrer's attitude to the Jews and to the 'Jewish problem'"! Gutsche not only facilitated the meeting with Sugihara but eventually gave Rabbi Zupnick a desk in the consulate to personally assist in the mammoth volume of paperwork for executing the visa applications. A special Gestapo mission to check on the Japanese intentions in opening the new consulate turned out to be one of the vital events for Torah survival and Jewish rescue!

In tribute to the humanitarianism of the Japanese consul, he was popularly called by the refugees "the Heaven-sent Angel of Salvation," and to his everlasting credit it must be stated that — in contrast to other consuls and influential people — he never accepted any gratuity for his exemplary humanitarian actions.

His distinguished actions found official recognition in a solemn ceremony at Yad Vashem, where he was awarded the "Righteous Gentile" award in 1985.

His wife, Yukoko Sugihara, accepted the award on behalf of her husband, as he was already too weak to undertake the journey to Jerusalem.

Other refugee groups and individuals from all walks of life followed in the footsteps of the Torah camp for their own rescue. They swelled the numbers of the Jewish refugees who left Russia through Vladivostok to about two thousand souls.

For Two Lit

The Lit was the national currency of Lithuania. There were five Lit to the dollar. For a mere two Lit, one could buy a visa and escape the Holocaust. This was the price charged by the Japanese consul for a Japanese transit visa. Only Heavenly Providence could offer a path to rescue with such smoothness and simplicity beyond any imagination.

But too many refused to apply for the Japanese and Curaçao visas. They thought, how could a visa for two Lit have any intrinsic value when all over the world consulates and diplomatic representatives offered visas for emigration and rescue to desperate European Jews for thousands of dollars apiece? They thought it was too simple and cheap to be taken seriously.

In spite of this, the bulk of the Polish-Lithuanian yeshivos, with many other war refugees, were miraculously saved by Russian Communist mass arrests of "unreliable elements" about one week before the German invasion of Russia. These new prisoners, now forcibly shipped to Siberia, were those who had disregarded the offer of the Japanese-Curaçao visa. While escaping the agonies of the Holocaust, their rescue entailed immeasurable torture and suffering in Siberia.

Under Duress

The Japanese visa was earmarked strictly "Transit through Japan" to a destination never to be arrived at by anyone of this group, because the end-visa to Curaçao was in itself a fiction created solely to obtain a Japanese transit visa. It was not the only fiction created out of desperation to save lives from danger. There were many more schemes and improvisations in some of the documents — with the utilization of the power of money — that came into being under the duress of persecutions, to result eventually in skillful counterfeits where needed.

Many of the people who belatedly joined the emigration efforts of various refugee groups had "missed the boat" for the Japanese transit visas, either because the Japanese consulate had already been closed or, earlier, when it refused to issue any more visas. Since they were convinced that nothing could be worse than life in Siberia, they took the lesser risk of attempting to forge Japanese visas. This was an extremely dangerous undertaking, especially since the would-be visa "artists" knew nothing about the nature of the Japanese symbols. A slight variation in an angle between two lines in a Japanese character could change the meaning of a word or a phrase. Nevertheless, the forged passports and prints had a surprisingly genuine appearance. After a while, the

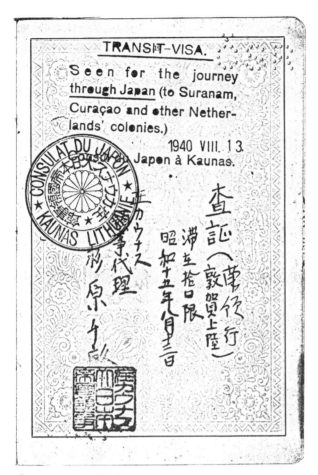

Japanese transit visa

refugees themselves learned to detect subtle discrepancies between official documents and forgeries. For example, the chrysanthemum of the genuine Japanese seal had one more petal — sixteen petals altogether — than those on the homemade documents. Strangely enough, this was never discovered by the Japanese themselves, who made a point of scrutinizing each travel document for ten to fifteen minutes before allowing the holder to pass. In fact, never was any forgery discovered which could have caused a change of attitude towards the group as a whole.

The Palm Reader

The long trek to freedom across continents was dotted with various minor and sometimes even exotic occurrences. They had no direct bearing on overall developments. Some incidents, however, are worthy of mention because they provided once-in-a-lifetime experiences.

The situation in Russian-occupied Eastern Europe was fraught with dangers of all kinds. Arrest, internal deportation and other punishments hung over every move. Earning money, possessing certain objects, holding certain opinions or having certain acquaintances could involve great risk. In this new life under the Russian regime, with its constant pressures, some relief was provided by an exotic source.

A talmudical student, hailing originally from Warsaw, had found a haven in the city of Vilna as a member of one of the smaller yeshiva groups. Here he started practicing the "science" of palm reading, foretelling from the lines of a person's palm future developments in that person's life.*

---

*Palm reading does not infringe on the religious prohibition against engaging in future-revealing schemes, as it is considered a solid discipline built on rules and experience, tested and proven by the initiated.

The Palm Reader

His palm reading techniques had been transmitted from father to son in his family for many generations.

Many, however, refused to consult this young palm reader on the secrets of their own future. If Heaven had cloaked the future under the raiment of the unknown, they felt it best not to uncover what Heaven kept beyond human knowledge.

This young man was so sure of his readings for his clients, that he requested payment in the form of a percentage of the profit of any newly established business undertaking for which he predicted success. His advice was also sought after in the non-business areas of human decision making and included some very successful matchmaking predictions.

Soviet regulations extended the validity of the newly issued exit visas to the entire family of the bearer. As the refugees grasped the potential of such a ruling, a ray of hope entered the life of many Lithuanian Jewish families. Soviet law had forced them — along with the rest of the population of the annexed Baltic states — to accept Soviet citizenship, which denied them the right to emigrate. Utilizing the provisions of the exit visa, many Lithuanian girls could theoretically leave Russia by consenting to "marry" in order to have their names entered as the spouse in the passport of an exit visa holder. But with a world at war and no place of refuge in sight, these young people were worried about the complications such a fictional marriage could lead to. Many of the "newlyweds" were fully aware that after being joined together on the passport for a time, the probability was quite high that the relationship would lead to marriage.

Since taking action on this issue could well affect the rest of one's life — after all, one was taking a risk in tying oneself legally to a stranger — a number of people turned for advice to the young palmist who was famous for his exceptionally successful advice. One of the younger members of the yeshiva group, a nineteen year old, approached the palm reader with his problem of "passport marriage." The palm reader took a glance at his palm and stepped back with an expression of shock and amazement. "You are still alive?" he said, more to himself than to his client. "Your life line is so short!" A year and a half later, the young man came down with typhoid fever in Shanghai, China, along with many others. All the victims recuperated except for him. He died at twenty-one.

Another scholar, today a prominent *rosh yeshiva* in America, was told: Don't get involved. In a year or two, you'll marry someone with the initials....Eventually he married in Shanghai, and his wife's name had the very initials that had been foretold.

Another student, later to become a well-known instructor and supervisor in an American yeshiva, was told more details: that his marriage would take place several years later and that he would have three children from that marriage, all of them boys. After he already had three sons, his wife became pregnant a fourth time. He related the prediction to his friends, showing how obviously inaccurate it was. Shortly afterwards, his wife miscarried. No further children were born to the couple.

Was the power of this palmist in reading the future enviable? The answer came forth in a tragic twist of life that only Providence can provide.

A few months after many Torah refugees had reached their haven, the city of Kobe in Japan, another trainload of refugee-emigrants, including a large number of passport-brides, reached their last stop on Russian territory, the Far Eastern port of Vladivostok, where they were placed under house arrest at the hotel where they were staying. Soviet authorities had become suspicious about the validity of the visas and final destination papers of the refugees.

The Palm Reader

Upon receipt of coded distress telegrams from Vladivostok, feverish rescue efforts started almost immediately in Kobe. Every possible attempt was made to obtain visas to new destinations. This necessiated obtaining large sums of money from America immediately in order to buy such visas from certain consulates.

Meanwhile, anxiety and despair reigned in the hallways and rooms of the Vladivostok *Intourist* hotel. Those detained by the Russians were faced with the threat of imprisonment and deportation to Siberia. The palm reader was also caught with this group. He did his best to help. He went from person to person, comforting and assuring, telling all of them that they would be saved. As for himself, he had read the writing on his own hand: he would be caught and deported to Siberia! At night he screamed in his dreams, "Father, Father, save me! Save me!" He walked around in despair. His reading again proved true. Every one of those detainees was ultimately permitted to leave for Japan — except him. The palm reader was arrested for carrying forged papers and exiled to Siberia.

Some people's refusal to consult the palm reader was motivated by concern for impairing their wholehearted faith in Divine Providence as demanded in Deuteronomy 18:13, while others shared the conviction that it is best "not to uncover what Heaven kept beyond human knowledge."

The ordeal of the palm reader was a tragic vindication of the latter attitude.

13

"On Eagles' Wings"

The escape route to Japan bore none of the earmarks of tragedy that characterized the struggle for rescue fought by the masses of European Jewry. The Torah refugees' phenomenal redemption from all potentially deadly encounters stood in striking contrast to the opposite manifestations of Divine Providence — at the very same places from which this group of Torah students could mercifully escape. In the historic centers of European Jewry, every flight from persecution was fraught with endless dangers and anxieties. But this group was lifted beyond the Holocaust at every stage of its escape from Europe, and in Asia as well. The direct line of the Trans-Siberian Railroad was their straight path of rescue. The amazing contrast between the fate decreed by Heaven for this small group and the fate of European Jewry as a whole was the most inexplicable phenomenon of the war. It was described by Rav Simcha Zelig Ryger, the *dayan* of Brisk, as being "above our intellect and understanding, and beyond human concepts."

Traveling on a railroad in a Communist country was not a right but a privilege. Without a special permit all inter-city travel, including the use of the railroad, was prohibited. No citizen was allowed to travel even within the country without a political investigation of his background by the secret police. Identity cards and travel permits were frequently checked on all trains. Railroad tickets could not be purchased without both documents. Consequently, an exit visa without the travel permit that entitled one to a railroad ticket served no purpose. The Soviet authorities were agreeable to the use of their trains for the departure, but there was one catch — the price.

The American dollar was then the oil that lubricated every war machine around the world. While an advance group of about twenty-five people had still been able to pay the regular fare in Russian rubles, the policy was changed immediately after. Tickets could only be purchased by partial payment in American dollars, and soon that was changed to "full dollar payment only."

The Communists, in accordance with their doctrine, tried to extract a maximum price from anyone making this final departure. This contributed to growing tension among the refugees, who were under ever-increasing pressure.

Each subsequent trainload of refugees had to pay a progressively higher fare. To add to the desperation and anxieties, a time limit was imposed on the later batches of exit visas. This meant that if the bearer could not obtain the necessary American dollars within the time limit, his precious visa would expire, which was tantamount to the cancellation of his hopes and dreams for a new life. Anyone holding an exit visa was therefore torn between the hope of escape and the nightmares of staying in Russia after the deadline as a declared enemy of the regime. This oscillation in the visa owners' state of mind perhaps explains why some of them had nervous breakdowns. Considering that the Russian ruble had lost almost all its value in those World War II days, how was a refugee to obtain the dollars he needed for saving his life?

When Orthodox Rabbis Desecrated the Sabbath

When the time limitation on the validity of the Russian exit visas was suddenly imposed, the Torah institutions sent pleas for help in desperate telegrams to America. Most were addressed to Rabbi Abraham Kalmanowitz, of blessed memory (later to become the dean of the Mirrer Yeshiva when it reestablished itself after the war), in New York. Rabbi Kalmanowitz, in cooperation with Orthodox Jewry's rabbinical and lay leaders, founded the rescue organization *Va'ad Hatzala*, which attempted to inform American Jewry of the events in Eastern Europe and of their significance for the survival of World Jewry. Rabbis, as well as laymen, teachers and students all threw themselves wholeheartedly and untiringly into the battle for rescue and Jewish survival. They endeavored to save these endangered Jewish lives by collecting large sums of money, and by interceding on their behalf with the highest United States Government officials and other Free World leaders in a gigantic rescue undertaking.

The imperative of saving human lives transcends almost every other commandment in Jewish law. During those crucial days and weeks, many people saw to their amazement venerable rabbis and religious leaders publicly desecrating the Sabbath in order to save lives. These were extreme and spectacular actions for Torah-true Jews; in order to gain precious time in their lifesaving efforts, they traveled on the Sabbath, rushing to any possible source of redemption. All endeavors were focused on this goal; there was no pausing, no resting in this noblest of all undertakings. Their efforts continued untiringly through day and night. Va'ad Hatzola encompassed every lifesaving activity. It became famous and revered for its breathtaking, globe-spanning endeavors even as World War II was spreading.

Visiting Friends in Moscow

During the many years of the notorious *chistkas* (purges) of the 1930s, when the Communists bloodily "purged" all those individuals they regarded as "unreliable," Premier Josef Stalin, through his dreaded secret police, the OGPU (a forerunner of the NKVD and the KGB), liquidated uncounted numbers of his supposed enemies from all levels of Communist society. Under his regime the last links of Russian Jewry with their families in other countries were severed, for any letter from a foreign country meant grave suspicion and potential danger for the Russian recipient. Not surprisingly, before the members of the yeshiva communities set out on their trans-Siberian trip, they were approached by many Lithuanian Jews who had lost contact with their families in Russia proper, and they were asked to convey regards or transmit letters to their relatives in the USSR, to make personal contact with them if possible, to learn more details about their situation, and eventually to relay such information to relatives abroad or back to Lithuania.

These contacts brought to light many heartbreaking stories about the disintegration of Russian Jewry. But such personal contact could not be made on the street during a visitor's stay in the capital. The omnipresent agents of the secret police were able to recognize a foreigner by the richness of his clothing and its different style; this contrasted sharply with drab, mass-produced Russian clothing. Any Russian spending more than a few moments with a foreigner exposed himself to suspicion and consequent surveillance. The visitor also had to be careful to avoid secret police agents who attempted to entrap specific foreigners. Whoever carried a message from relatives outside of Russia had to locate the family and visit them personally in their apartment.

A further obstacle to close contact was the fact that a multitude of people commonly shared the same apartment. Houses and apartments in Russia belonged to the "people." Every person was allotted a certain number of square feet of living space within a given apartment which had to be shared with others. The lack of privacy was not only dehumanizing but also dangerous, as every dweller was spied upon by all the others for the benefit of the state.

In one case, a member of the yeshiva community eventually located the Moscow home of the sister of an acquaintance in Lithuania. He was met at the door by a number of people. Finally, the person for whom the visitor was inquiring arrived at the door. Surprised and fearful, she did not extend an invitation to enter. She was a relatively young woman, being the younger sister of the visitor's acquaintance in Lithuania, but her white hair and the furrows of sorrow that lined her face bore testimony to a life of hardship and suffering. She asked the visitor to return after nine o'clock that evening.

The brief conversation late that evening explained why the woman had aged so prematurely. She had chosen that hour for the meeting because then her only child would be away from the room, to attend a Communist Party youth meeting. She had lost many members of her close family, one by one. First her father-in-law had been deported because he was a rabbi, then the mother-in-law because she was a rabbi's wife. Husband and wife were deported separately and not to the same camp in Siberia so that they should not have the comfort of being together and consoling each other. (At that time, it was the policy of the Communist system to keep victims isolated from family.) Later, they arrested this woman's husband too; his crime was that he was a rabbi's son. "My hair grew all white during those years of suffering without end," she told the visitor.

"All I have left is my only son. They turned him into my most dangerous enemy. They have indoctrinated him to believe that his parents are parasites and enemies of society, criminals and foes of the people. He is expected as his noblest achievement to spy on me and report regularly on what I say and do. That's why I had to avoid talking to you earlier and ask you to return at this time, when my son would be away at his Komsomol meeting."

From Vilna to Vladivostok with Torah Luminaries

For almost two hundred thousand Jews from Russian-occupied Poland, a trip on the Trans-Siberian Railroad was a trip to doom in one of the many slave labor camps that dot the map of Siberia. The exile of so large a part of Polish Jewry to Siberia was one of the great tragedies of Jewish history. In the impenetrable forests and in endless snow-covered wastes of the Arctic region, the deportees were exposed to icy storms at minus fifty degrees Fahrenheit. Other slave laborers, transported to the dry, hot steppes of Kazakhstan and Samarkand, suffered indescribable misery that often ended in sickness and death.

Those familiar with the harsh facts of life under the Stalinist regime find it inconceivable that this special group of about two thousand refugees, comprising the camp of Torah scholars and originating from the very same lands of Jewish suffering, was allowed to cross the dreaded Siberian regions on the same tracks, not as slave laborers but as travelers treated with the courtesies reserved for official tourists and guests. They crossed Siberia in "Russian-style" travel luxury. (Accommodations were by no means luxurious by Western standards; instead of soft plush seats, there were simple, sturdy wooden benches on each side of a coach compartment.) This contrast, in terms of Heavenly Providence, was startling. Swerdlovsk, Chelyabinsk, Irkutsk, Novosibirsk, and many other Siberian cities that are the fruits of slave labor, of human misery, were pointed out by Russian travel "guides" to these yeshiva groups — who now were full-fledged "tourists" — as "miracles of Russian technology and industrial development."

There was also a striking contrast between the conduct of the yeshiva passengers and that of the other people on those trains. In the words of a western European fellow passenger who was unaware of the unique status of the scholars and Torah giants with whom he lived for two weeks on the Trans-Siberian train:

> *They showed a puzzling kind of conduct all day, constantly arguing with each other — but in friendship! Quarreling and disputing, even in larger groups — but only verbally! Their heated disputes focused on oversized books, large bulky volumes from which the disputes seemed to originate or to end.*

As striking as this observation might seem about the manner in which the remnants of the famous European Torah centers spent their days on the trans-Siberian trains, that observer could barely appreciate the high scholastic and religious standards of his fellow travelers, who spent their days of miraculous rescue in the study of Torah. They were absorbed in trying to solve numerous problems of legal, ethical and religious character arising out of the changing conditions and the technical innovations they were encountering during this trip. These new facts had to be assessed according to the principles of Torah living. The heated debates were testimony to the depth of commitment of those individuals to the obligations and principles of Torah life.

Many of the *halachic* problems discussed during the

two-week journey across Asia centered on Sabbath observance. Among the questions that arose: was it permissible on the Sabbath to discharge objects from inside the train to the outside, such as when flushing toilet facilities? Another question explored: was it permissible on the Sabbath to raise the wall ledges that formed the back of the compartment's seat and were pulled out from the walls into a new horizontal position, forming a new top floor that provided the base for the upper berth on which people slept at night? Simultaneously a new "ceiling" was thus formed above the person lying on the bench below.

The participants in these disputes included famous experts on Jewish law and heads of yeshivos — such world-renowned scholars as Rabbi Reuven Grozovsky, Rabbi Aharon Kotler, Rabbi Yechezkel Levenstein, Rabbi Chayim Shmuelevitz and many present day Torah luminaries.

(L.) Rabbi Chayim Shmuelevitz, Mirrer Rosh Yeshiva; (r.) Rabbi Yechezkel Levenstein, Mirrer Mashgiach

A New Hunger in a Hungry Land

Aside from making individual contacts with Russian Jews on a personal basis, many of the travelers had a strong desire to meet Russian Jews within the framework of a Jewish community. An opportunity for such an encounter offered itself when the refugee transports passed through the Amur River region, near the Far Eastern border of the USSR. Here, under the pretext of giving its Jewish population the same rights as other minorities, the Russian government had promised the Jews an autonomous state of their own, named Birobidzhan. Many thousands of Jews had settled in that "promised land" where they helped tap and cultivate the unexploited resources of that Far Eastern wilderness.

But all the rosy promises of the Soviet government proved to be nothing but empty lies, skillfully planned to exploit the yearning of the Jews for a homeland. It had served the military planning of the Communist regime to lure Jews to that desolate region in order to strengthen its border positions in the Far East against a possible military confrontation with its Eastern neighbors, especially against an expansionist Japan. Many Jews subsequently tried to escape from there. What had begun as a struggle against the hardships of climate and nature turned into a life of torment, deprivation and abandonment.

According to the guiding principles of government-controlled Soviet tourism, travelers were to be kept away from Birobidzhan and its population, lest the truth about the "autonomous Jewish republic" reach the outside world. Intourist, the official government travel bureau that conducts all trips within Russia, assigned guides and companions to the foreigners in order to create positive propaganda for the Communist regime and to keep the visitors from coming in contact with unfavorable aspects of life in the Soviet Union. These agents supervised every move of the foreign travelers. But on the long, two-week trip with the Trans-Siberian Railroad, some of the guides succumbed to the temptation to fraternize with the refugee travelers and accepted occasional small bribes. In confidential conversations they admitted that they were personally responsible for preventing any individual in the group from coming into contact with objects that were officially supposed to remain "unseen." The itinerary planned for each visitation included only those sightseeing spots that supported the aims of Soviet propaganda. "To show only such places was the distinctive mark of a skillful propagandist-guide," they explained.

The Intourist guides officially announced that no passengers would be allowed to get off when the train made a stop at Birobidzhan's railroad station. The stop, they claimed, would be so short that anyone who got off might find himself left behind.

But the temptation to see the lot of Birobidzhan's Jews for themselves was too great! Some people left the train in spite of all these warnings. At the station platform itself they found the local population, who met the trains to beg for food. After the first transports of the Jewish "tourists" passed by, word circulated, and more locals met the trains to make contact with the Jews on subsequent transports.

This hunger that the travelers encountered in Birobidzhan was a different kind of hunger than they had met at the many stops throughout Siberia. Previously the impoverished population, adults and children, dressed in rags, begged tourists for food or clothing until they were finally chased away by the police. The tourists had been told that these people were gypsies or other undesirables who spurned honest work, preferring to live as parasites "off other people's goodness."

But here in Birobidzhan the refugees encountered a very different kind of poverty — not a hunger for food and clothing, but a spiritual hunger. As the Birobidzhan Jews recognized the Jewish group, they besieged them for "lifesaving staples." The refugees were begged to leave behind *taleisim*, prayerbooks, Jewish calendars and Bibles. The Jews of Birobidzhan were more insistent in their requests than all the supplicants the travelers had met at many other stations. These Jews argued that the travelers could always buy replacements for their own needs, once they arrived in the Free World. They on the other hand, were condemned to stay at "home," in Birobidzhan, cut off from any source that supplied them with the basics of Jewish living, and therefore they had a greater claim to such items. These were heart-rending, irresistible appeals from the depths of Jewish suffering.

For the travelers it was hard to suppress the desire to see more of their brethren and to gain additional intimate knowledge of their lives in order to help them. However, the "tourists" were forewarned by their coreligionists at the railroad station not to make any attempt to leave the station to explore life beyond it. But the Jewish feelings were too strong to be restrained, and some of the more audacious tried the "impossible." Those who left the station and slipped into the city were, after some success in their adventurous explorations, eventually apprehended.

A New Hunger in a Hungry Land

Both the organized supervision of citizens in Russia and the difference in the travelers' clothing contributed to their discovery. Sooner or later those travelers were stopped, questioned and arrested.

There were no civil liberties for the individual in the autocratic Soviet regime. Walking around on public streets, traveling, working, were all privileges granted by the state. As "guests," tourists received preferential treatment and were not put in the city jail, but were placed under house arrest in a hotel.

Initially, judging from the rough, wooden walls, covered only in part with remnants of tattered and faded wallpaper, the travelers were sure they were in a prison. Only later did they realize that their quarters were indeed the guest rooms of the only hotel in town. Such was the standard of living in the city of Birobidzhan, the capital of the "autonomous" region of Birobidzhan.

Those few "law-breaking" refugees were lucky. The authorities treated them gently, like foreign travelers who had gotten lost while on a trip. After being interrogated they were put on an airplane so that they could catch up with their group at the next but distant railroad station, Khabarovsk. As an aftermath to this incident, the Russians ordered later trains bearing additional groups of Jewish "refugee tourists" not to stop at all at the Birobidzhan railroad station.

During the stopover in the Birobidzhan train station, as at all the other stops en route, the travelers observed the repetition of another most impressive phenomenon: the disbelief and wonder in the eyes of the people at seeing others actually leaving Russia — leaving the empire of many nations for whom there is no out. The words "leaving Russia" sounded to them like a fairy tale. The mere idea of leaving the Communist paradise was unthinkable. A few seconds before getting off the train at

Operation: Torah Rescue

one of the stations, a Russian army colonel asked abruptly, "How long will a free world witness the enslavement of two hundred million people and keep silent?" Then he walked quickly away.

This group of Jewish refugee-travelers who traversed the steppes of Siberia were the beneficiaries of the greatest gift the Soviets could ever bestow on any of their citizens — the gift of a new life in the outside world — to be able to breathe sweet, sweet freedom again.

Vladivostok

The most important Far Eastern Russian city was Vladivostok, the eastern terminal of the Trans-Siberian railway line, a port city on the Sea of Japan. During their stay there the refugees were eager to meet average Soviet citizens to learn more about life in the Russian Far East. But, again, it was extremely difficult to approach anyone because of the ever-present secret police and because people were afraid to be seen talking to anyone so obviously foreign as these travelers in their foreign clothing. Only occasional remarks from some Russian citizens provided sudden insights into the underlying tensions among the populace.

The only real contact the refugees were able to establish with Russians was with other travelers lodged in their Intourist hotel. Most of these Russian travelers who were accorded travel permits were the most favored individuals of the Soviet system — actors.

Actors were carefully nurtured by the Soviet system because their performances and talents were powerful tools in extolling the achievements of the Communist system and for influencing all spheres of public and private life with Communist doctrine. The performers were lavishly paid and considered among the most affluent citizens of the USSR. Of course, all their wealth could not buy them many of the consumer goods they desired, as these simply were not available in the Russia of Stalinist priorities.

Ample confirmation of these conditions could be found in a visit to the giant, government-run department store of Vladivostok, the main outlet for the purchase of manufactured goods. It revealed an incomplete assortment of drab and rather poorly displayed merchandise. But the most depressing feature of the store was the general shortage of merchandise. The little that was available was often useless because, in many instances, parts or complementing articles that were supposed to go with them were missing. For instance, if there was thread, there were no needles, or vice versa. This was true for many of the consumer goods; it was a typical by-product of the Communist system that lacked all incentives for human enterprise. As a result of this shortage, money had relatively little value in Russia.

It turned out that movie stars, the darlings of the Soviet system, were ready to pay the foreign travelers fantastic amounts of money even for used or worn consumer articles. They paid one hundred and fifty dollars for an inexpensive man's wristwatch. For an eight-dollar pair of shoes they offered one hundred dollars, grateful to be able to purchase it! And one must realize that the dollar was worth much more in 1941!

Such friendly "bargain hunting" gave rise to informal conversation about life in the Soviet Union as opposed to that in the Western world. Strangely enough, the refugees' description of economic and social conditions elsewhere, of Free World prices and wages, and the access of their population to the luxuries of life, made little impression on the actors. Their life experience in the Soviet Union had conditioned them from early childhood to consider what we would call hardships, such as having to stand in long lines for a loaf of bread, to be the *normal* way of life. In fact, Soviet life was accepted by them to such a degree that descriptions of conditions for the masses in the Western world sounded as fantastic to them as fairy tales of lands where gold rained down from heaven. To them such a life was the exception rather than the rule. So it did not even arouse in them the desire to try to obtain it for themselves.

A Narrow Escape from Shipwreck

Vladivostok is Russia's gateway to the Pacific. During the years immediately preceding World War II there was little traffic over the seaways between the Soviet Far East and neighboring Japan. Japan was concentrating all her efforts on an expansionist war against China. There was only one small steamship, the 2,500-ton *Amakuza Maru*, that made the thirty-six-hour crossing each week between Vladivostok and Tsuruga, a small fishing port on the Japanese main island of Honshu. The *Amakuza Maru* was a relatively small ship to sail the Sea of Japan, one of the world's most turbulent bodies of water. But its facilities were more than ample for the small number of travelers who slipped in and out through the port of Vladivostok, Russia's back door.

But now, with the constant arrival of refugee transports in Vladivostok, the *Amakuza Maru* suddenly was catapulted into a historic mission of rescue, being the much-sought-after means of travel. As the remnants of Torah Jewry escaped from the European continent, hundreds upon hundreds of men, women and children dangerously overloaded the small ship on its weekly trips through the notoriously stormy sea. The ship's cabins were no longer sufficient to accommodate everyone, and passengers

A Narrow Escape from Shipwreck

unable to find cabins were forced to lie on the deck.

The small ship was tossed about on the stormy seas like a ball, battered by waves as high as a house. At times the steamer listed to its side, almost parallel to the water's surface, so that it was impossible for the passengers to get up from the ship's floor. Besides, the passengers had been packed on board like sardines in a can — in total disregard of safety regulations. In the extraordinarily heavy storm winds, no lifeboats could be lowered; even the life belts available were useless under such adverse conditions. The first night of this author's voyage, he noticed the captain and crew counting the passengers. It was determined that there were not enough life belts, and lifeboat seats could be assigned only to women and children. Besides the extreme danger to life that prevailed on this and similar trips, there was also great misery on board the ship due to the seasickness that many of the passengers suffered from throughout the stormy passage.

When the boat finally landed at the port of Tsuruga, the special blessing of thanksgiving and praise to the Almighty for the rescue from the dangers of crossing the sea was recited by all the men with unusual and grateful fervor. They were joyful at having survived a most dangerous and fearful crossing, when the boat with its precious human cargo was tossed up and down the valleys and peaks of the towering waves.

But the extent of the miracle on these dangerous crossings was only later fully driven home to the refugees.

Once the last shipload of refugees from Russia had reached the shores of the Japanese islands, the *Amakuza Maru* had finally completed a historic mission of Heavenly mercy and rescue, ferrying out the last refugees from Russia to the port of Tsuruga in Japan. It had achieved a triumph of historic dimensions.

On one of the ship's later passages from Russia without

A group of refugees arriving in Japan

refugees on board, it met with the catastrophe that it had narrowly escaped so often before, despite its overload of refugees. On its final journey, having booked only a few passengers for the Tsuruga home port, the *Amakuza Maru* just broke apart under the onslaught of nature. One more of the tremendous miracles at every stage of rescue had been revealed.

The horrendous experience of crossing one of the world's stormiest seas made many scrutinize with new awareness the miracle of the apparent normality and tranquility of the initial part of the escape from Russia by way of the Trans-Siberian Railroad. The protective, tourist-like arrangement was another miraculous aspect of the rescue process. The Biblical verse of the Gaon of Vilna's lot "I will carry you on eagles' wings and will bring you close to Me" (Exodus 19:4), which provided crucial encouragement in Kovno for undertaking the journey, had by now acquired a special ring of fulfillment in many minds.

Japanese Hospitality

The hospitality extended to the Jewish refugees by the Japanese, both individually and officially — as part of Japan's national policy toward the influx of white refugees from Soviet Russia — was a splendid display of human compassion. Japan showed a great deal of understanding and benevolence to these groups of Jewish refugees — despite its agreement with Nazi Germany to foment anti-Semitic hatred as a kind of "cultural achievement" in its national life.

The refugees remained well protected from all dire consequences of Nazi plans and Nazi pressure on Japan* throughout the nine months they spent there; perhaps this was because the anti-Semitic stereotype of a Jew was still an alien concept to the Japanese. A giant-size drawing of the "Hated Jew" from the infamous German hate journal, *Der Stürmer*, was mounted on the front of one of Tokyo's largest department stores. The "portrait" covered the entire wall from the third to the tenth floor of the building's street front, but it meant nothing to the

---

*See Marvin Tokayer and Mary Swartz, *Desperate Voyagers* (New York: Dell Publishing Co., 1980), 237-55, which discloses details of the annihilation plans.

passersby in the street, because the average Japanese had never met a Jew, and those few who had made contact with Jews did not identify them with the caricature presented of them as the "source of all evil" in the world. To most Japanese, the Jew of the poster looked like one of the Indian Sikhs who, as members of the Colonial British Police, were a common sight in many parts of the Far East.

On the official level, the Japanese hospitality was also demonstrated when the authorities created no difficulties about extending the refugees' transit visas — although it was by then no longer a secret that the Japanese transit visas had been granted on the basis of an erroneous assumption that there existed a "final destination," Curaçao. The governor of Curaçao had contested the validity of those visas, so the Japanese transit visa became a de facto end-visa.

Their new status was regarded by the refugee group as yet another manifestation of the Heavenly guidance for the Torah community. In the Japanese city of Kobe, guided, supported, and protected by the exemplary hospitality of the local community of Russian and Sephardic Jews with American support — the refugees established a House of Torah for their studies, and Kobe became the center for living and learning for the continuously arriving shiploads of refugees.

During their stay in Japan, many refugees, especially those without affiliation to yeshivos, endeavored to obtain visas to other lands or certificates to Palestine. Many succeeded, including Dr. Zerach Warhaftig, who was a central figure in the many rescue and migration efforts concerning the refugees. He later became Minister of Religions in the State of Israel.

What else but constant Heavenly protection can explain the strange actions of the Imperial Japanese Foreign Secretary, Yosuke Matsuoka? Although an architect of the tripartite Axis Powers treaty, he personally became instrumental in extending the refugees' now questionable "transit" visas far beyond their initial term of two weeks — through discreet instructions to the Kobe Police Prefecture and with the tacit approval of his government* — thus practically transforming them into end-visas!

The remaining refugees realized the danger to themselves should Japan enter World War II on the side of the Axis Powers and against the Allies and assorted governments-in-exile whose citizens they were. But in spite of these clouds on the political horizon during the tension-filled pre-Pearl Harbor days, they maintained their faith and confidence that they were being guarded by Heavenly Providence.

Eventually, the Japanese authorities grew impatient with the refugees stranded in Kobe with only transit visas and nowhere to go. Three months before Pearl Harbor, they decided to deport them to occupied China, where they were dumped into the free city of Shanghai. The yeshiva community, however, regarded this again as another act of Divine grace, as they were spared the fate of other foreign civilians in Japan, who after Pearl Harbor were rounded up and placed in internment camps.

They also saw their deportation to China as a welcome solution for certain religious problems concerning Sabbath and *Yom Kippur* observance which they had to contend with on the Japanese islands. These were the results of conflicting *halachic* views regarding the location of the international dateline, which was established in the

---

*See the autobiography of Matsuoka's private secretary, Professor Setzuso Abraham Kotsuji, *From Tokyo to Jerusalem* (New York: Bernard Geis Assoc., 1964).

middle of the uninhabited Pacific Ocean by European consensus, purely for reasons of convenience. Torah law draws the dateline to coincide with the geographical longitudinal line where the first day of Creation started to dawn — while darkness still prevailed to the east of it! *Halachic* authorities disagree as to where this line is located. When arguments involve the observance of Sabbath law, the *halacha* may require keeping certain Sabbath laws for two days instead of one, in specific areas on both sides of the disputed line. The problem as to the exact location of the *halachic* dateline led to the question of whether the Japanese islands are east or west of this dateline, resulting in a dispute about identifying the Sabbath day on the Japanese islands. These *halachic* disputes, with their resulting problems, led many refugees to set aside a two-day Sabbath for various degrees of Sabbath observance! Also, while one group of scholars would recite *kiddush*, welcoming the Sabbath, on Saturday night, another group simultaneously observed the *havdala* ceremony, in farewell to the departing Sabbath!

The controversies among the scholars over the true Sabbath day in Japan would become theoretical once the deported refugees arrived on the Chinese mainland which, as part of the Euro-Asian continent, had no *halachic* ambiguity. The move occurred just in time, before the need arose to confront the problem of which day to observe the Yom Kippur fast day.

Actually a small group *was* still left in Japan at the arrival of Yom Kippur. The members of the group were faced with the hardship of fasting two days consecutively. Some of them observed two days of complete Yom Kippur fasting, while the others kept the fast for just one day and on the other day followed certain *halachic* modifications for fasting under such circumstances.

An Encounter with Idols and Idol Worship

Life in Japan, as the refugees learned, is a strange mixture of ancient customs and beliefs with modern science. For individuals from Western cultures, idolatry is a phenomenon of history, unknown in detail, except to scholars of the Bible, of the Talmud, or of ancient history. In Japan, many scholars among the refugees were surprised to discover these remnants of antiquity still in practice. A large part of the Japanese population practiced Buddhism and Shintoism, and also the worship of some 168,000 idols. This first-hand experience with the phenomenon of historic paganism was for many of the scholars the discovery of a lifetime. They were greatly surprised to note that the proverbial "holy cow" became in Japan "holy sheep," grazing in the gardens of the temples and worshiped by the people.

An incident that illustrated those ancient concepts of idol worship involved an elderly peasant couple who approached the statue of a rotund idol. The white-haired farmer and his aged wife placed a tray filled with fruits and cereals squarely before the idol. Then, apparently after reciting some prayers, they left the shrine and its surrounding garden.

At nightfall, shadowy figures entered the garden from

85

the rear. They closed in from the back of the statue, and after a short pause, one by one they stretched out their hand to reach around to the front of the god. The young priests in their tight black robes quickly snatched object after object from the tray and refreshed themselves with the delicious offerings to the idol. In no time the tray was emptied of all its delicacies.

Next morning, a curious Jewish scholar lingered at the site and observed a touching scene. The old couple arrived at the gardens and approached the statue of the idol-god, expectantly straining to catch a glimpse of the tray. They hurried towards the corpulent god. The tray was really empty! The pair's happiness knew no bounds. They embraced each other in ecstasy over their wonderful good fortune — that the god was pleased with their gift and had graciously accepted and completely consumed it. It was a scene out of ancient history, a replay of antiquity from the forgotten ages of Biblical times, at the beginning of mankind.

The Japanese and the Ten Lost Tribes

A legend is maintained among Japanese that a segment of the Japanese people are descendants of the lost tribes of Israel. As evidence, they cite names of several places in Japan, one allegedly named Joseph and another named Goshen, and many minor details that traditional Shintoism shares with ancient Judaism.

The attitude of these "relatives" toward various Jewish refugees was one of special sympathy. The refugees received many favors from such Japanese citizens. One member of the Japanese intelligentsia, Professor Setzuso Kotsuji, then secretary to the Japanese foreign minister, provided special assistance to the refugees in dealing with Japanese officialdom. In a foreign country with unknown customs and procedures, with a psychology inscrutable to Westerners, such an intermediary was vital to the refugees in their dealings with the authorities. The sympathy and friendliness of Professor Kotsuji to the refugees reached its climax many years later when Professor Kotsuji converted to Judaism, joining the faith and accepting the destiny of the Jewish people. He adopted the name Abraham Kotsuji and lived for a time in Brooklyn, New York, the largest Jewish community in the world. But in accordance with his wishes, he was brought to his final rest in the eternal city of

Prof. S. Kotsuji

Tombstone of Prof. Abraham Kotsuji, brought to his final rest in Jerusalem

At the reception in the Mirrer Yeshiva, Jerusalem.
Prof. Abraham Kotsuji; (seated, to his left) Rabbi Chayim Shmuelevitz

the Jewish people, Jerusalem. His funeral in the Holy City was attended by many of the former refugees who had been stranded in Japan, and also by Dr. Zerach Warhaftig, the Minister of Religions of the State of Israel at the time of the funeral. Scholars and members of the faculty of the Mirrer Yeshiva in Jerusalem were among the famous participants in this unique funeral.

The Free Port of Shanghai

Nine months of Japanese hospitality in 1941 came to an abrupt end when the military preparations for Pearl Harbor neared their climax. It was to be expected that the large group of refugees, composed of citizens from countries at war with the Axis powers, would be viewed with extreme suspicion following Japan's secret decision to enter World War II on the side of the Axis. Deporting the refugees to Shanghai was the natural solution.

The free city of Shanghai, into which the Torah scholars and their institutions were tossed, was truly free from obligations to any law — free and open to the homeless, the exiled, the outcasts and the hunted criminals from all over the globe. Whoever desired to enter its gates found free access and a haven. In such an atmosphere, devoid of restrictions of any kind, could a yeshiva community — followers of a law code that regulates every step in life — sink roots and grow the sublime products of Torah ideals? Having been saved miraculously for the sake of upholding their ideals and studies, could they maintain their lifestyle in such an environment? Or would their devotion to Torah principles weaken in such an isolated corner of the world, surrounded by exotic cultures and strange forms of civilization?

The answer was never really in doubt. Steadfastness to their Jewish ideals and principles was at the root of the refugees' miraculous escape from the centers of the Holocaust and their eventual arrival in the remote Far East.

To illustrate the exotic dimensions of this globe-spanning odyssey of the yeshiva community: only one year earlier this author had asked the spiritual leader of the Mirrer Yeshiva, Rabbi Yechezkel Levenstein, whether it would be advisable for him personally to flee to Shanghai. The rabbi was completely flabbergasted at the selection of China for a place of refuge. After his initial surprise, he explained that Shanghai would be unacceptable because of the host of difficulties an individual would face in trying to maintain a Torah way of life there by himself. Yet, barely one year later, the Torah community's House of Study had arrived at that same exotic place — Shanghai!

Of course, there were countless worries: how and where to find acceptable housing, how to support organized religious life and studies on the level demanded by these standard-bearers of Torah. How could the rabbis with their families, and the hundreds of students, find the bare necessities of life in this overcrowded Chinese seaport and commercial center? Where would they find a building adequate to house the students and provide study halls and all the necessary supporting facilities for so many people?

But the impossible once again became reality. All their problems were solved as soon as they landed in Shanghai! The entire Mirrer Yeshiva group was placed in a single synagogue, an extraordinary synagogue with unusual facilities in an odd location that had been built by an eccentric individual under the strangest of circumstances. It was the solution to all of the refugees' problems and needs, and it made possible five years of the most creative Torah studies for the yeshiva community, within a most suitable setup, in far distant China.

This edifice, the Beis Aharon or Museum Road Synagogue, stood in a strange location for a synagogue — in the very heart of Shanghai's port and business district near the famous Bund, the docking area for all ships. This synagogue had stood empty and almost unused for the first ten years after its erection, except for occasional prayer sessions and wedding ceremonies or as a temporary emergency shelter, until the day of the yeshiva's arrival. The synagogue was a modern structure and contained a sanctuary built to meet all requirements of religious law. Strangely, the number of seats in the synagogue, 250, corresponded to the number of yeshiva students who would study there.

In addition to the main sanctuary, the building contained large dining rooms and kitchen facilities. It had been built to meet the needs of a residential community and contained all the facilities for catering services, including halls for wedding celebrations and other communal affairs. But no such nearby Jewish community existed in Shanghai until the arrival of the yeshiva scholars. The building provided for their spiritual and physical needs to an amazing degree. In a building adjoining the synagogue there was even a *mikveh*, which complemented the synagogue facility to almost supreme perfection.

Who was the thoughtful sponsor of this veritable palace of Jewishness in the Far East? An outstanding rabbi? A deeply religious businessman? A famous community worker or philanthropist?

Heavenly Providence revealed itself in an apparently miraculous manifestation by choosing the seemingly most unworthy and inappropriate person to build this place of refuge for Torah. In fact, this Jew was so estranged from his own religion that he had married a non-Jewish woman!

The Beis Aharon Synagogue on Museum Road, Shanghai. (Beth Hatefutsoth Archive)

For minds addicted to rationalization and explanations, prominence might be given to the book *Escape to Shanghai*.* It says that the rich donor, Silas Hardoon, was motivated by a dream to build this edifice. He chose such a non-residential section on the basis of plans for a future Jewish neighborhood in the area. Silas Hardoon had, of course, never earmarked these buildings for a school for the teaching and practice of Jewish law. Nevertheless, he carried out his "mission" with almost perfect planning to fit perfectly the specific purpose and needs of the group of Torah scholars who landed a decade later on the shores of China. These inexplicable facts transcend any calculations or fantasies of the human mind. Again unbelievable circumstances had led to the rescue and continuation of Torah study.

---

* *Escape to Shanghai*, 69-70.

Study hall of Museum Road Synagogue (Beis Aharon), Shanghai, 1941. (Far left) Rabbi Yechezkel Levenstein, Mashgiach; (far right) Rabbi Joseph Epstein, Secretary; (second from right) Rabbi Chayim Shmuelevitz, Rosh Yeshiva

For almost five years, these buildings housed the centers of Jewish thinking and scholarship. These were some of the most fruitful years in Torah research and history, years that left deep and lasting effects on the spiritual growth of almost every participant. In fact, it may even be fair to say that many rabbis and communal leaders who later became famous on the American continent owe

their spiritual achievements in large measure to those productive years of studies in China.

There were two other yeshiva communities which were significant among the Torah scholars. They constituted, albeit on a smaller scale, their former yeshivos: the Lubavitch Yeshiva and the Lublin Yeshiva. The structure of their studies and their focus on *Chassidic* teachings and mode of living required a separate yeshiva setup for these students. They therefore gathered in study halls and student living complexes of their own.

A number of factors contributed to make those years in Shanghai especially fruitful. The gnawing uncertainties of being completely isolated from one's own family and disconnected from Jewish life the world over made these scholars immerse themselves in their studies with greater fervor than ever before. The fact that they knew themselves to be on an "island of rescue" at a time when horrifying destruction engulfed the former centers of Jewish culture, imposed on them even greater obligations to the God Who saved and guarded them. The bustling atmosphere and the myriad distractions of the metropolis of Shanghai — a tremendous center of world commerce, being the gateway to China with hundreds of millions populating its hinterland — could not penetrate these chambers of study. In the courts of the Museum Road Synagogue, its study hall and prayer center, Jewish study and research went on with more fervor than ever.

(Constant Heavenly protection revealed itself again when, after an initial period of hunger caused by temporary post-Pearl Harbor changes, Shanghai emerged again as a city abundant in foodstuffs and general merchandise.)

Other unexpected blessings were the technological innovations created by Shanghai's unique printing industry. The Torah community was completely shut off from the world on which it had always depended for its books and other resources to foster its spiritual life and studies. The armadas of the warring world powers sealed off all the sea lanes for delivery of such vital supplies. But rescue came again for the spiritual endeavors of the yeshivos. Shanghai's political climate, diametrically opposed to the teachings of Torah laws, unexpectedly furnished its solution.

Of all the port cities of the world, the city of Shanghai

was the queen of lawlessness. The word "lawlessness" is inadequate here, because no law was meaningful in Shanghai except for "the law of dispensing graft." Bribery of all minor and high-ranking officials, from the policeman on the street to the presiding judge in court, was the way of life. Business, uninhibited by restrictions, was unlimited in scope. There were no set hours for business, and many stores were open till midnight, seven days a week. In such an unrestricted business climate, special industries sprang up.

One of them was Shanghai's new printing industry for the mass reproduction of copyrighted works from all over the world. "Pirating" flourished in Shanghai, for the laws of the free city did not give recognition to the international convention of copyright laws. For the purpose of reproducing and exploiting the cultural treasures of the world, the new industry found a system to reprint those books in a most inexpensive way. The Chinese invention of the special process, "Shanghai lithography," used a type of stone treated with inexpensive chemicals, which made possible the reprinting of unlimited numbers of copies by this special process.

Books are the tools for transmitting the cultural values of Judaism in yeshivos all over the world. They are the obsession and the lifeline of Jewish scholars. A very few of the Shanghai refugee community, blessed with enterprising idealism, utilized their presence in the one city in the world that had created this unique industry in order to reproduce printed treasures from the world of Talmud and Judaica. By using the Chinese printing process to good advantage, they rebuilt and extended communal and individual libraries to include all the basic works of Jewish culture. From single copies of books saved by individual students, complete sets of textbooks, including whole parts of Talmud, were reproduced. Thus,

Operation: Torah Rescue

scholars were enabled not only to replenish all original sources of books and publications needed for the yeshiva studies, but also to extend the scope of their spiritual progress. And, for the first time in Jewish history, there appeared Jewish books bearing the legend "Printed in China" on the bottom of the title page. Most important, this "first" meant that the yeshiva community could now continue its Jewish studies, even on the far-off shores of China.

A farewell party for Rabbi Osher Lichtstein, Rabbi Shmuel (Charkower) Wilensky and others leaving for the U.S.A. and Canada. On the table are copies of the journal "Torah Or", which had just been completed in memory of Rabbi Avrohom Arbus, a fellow student. Seated: (l. to r.) Rabbis Joel Rosen, Zelig Kirzner, Avrohom Dovid Niznik, Osher Lichtstein, Shmuel (Charkower) Wilensky, Jacob Finkelstein, Nochum Perzovitz, Shmuel Birnbaum. Standing: Zvi Kahane, Nochum Lesman, Boruch Rosenberg, Moshe Bick, Dovid Kastrovitzky, Moshe Pitterman, Avrohom Aron Serebrowski, Moshe Bunim Pirotinsky, Shmuel Eli Orlanski, Moshe Leizersohn, Sholom Shapiro, Jacob Maggid, Reuben Fein, Moshe Eisenberg, Aron Kreiser, Hershel Zarkowsky.

Title page of Rambam's Mishneh Torah, reprinted by the Mirrer Yeshiva in Shanghai

PRINTED IN SHANGHAI

War Expanding to the Far East

The attackers of Pearl Harbor had included the white-race students of the yeshiva community in their detailed planning. Three months before the attack, they had forced them into an exodus to rid the Japanese home island of any potential white spies. Thus the yeshiva students found themselves already in Shanghai when war in the Pacific suddenly broke out.

Shock waves of Pearl Harbor reached Shanghai earlier than most places. When it was dawn on December 7, 1941, at Pearl Harbor — about midnight in Shanghai — heavy Japanese artillery opened fire on a lone American gunboat anchored on the Whangpoo River. The thunderous pounding of heavy artillery jolted the population out of their sleep. The refugees immediately ventured various guesses as to the origins of these explosions. Some of the yeshiva students who had served in the Polish army during the German invasion of Poland correctly attributed the sounds to heavy ship artillery. When the U.S. Marines aboard the gunboat rejected the Japanese call for surrender, a short but sharp duel between unequal fire power eliminated the last real U.S. military power on the Asian continent.

A few hours later, at daybreak, truckloads of Japanese

soldiers crossed the borders of the various Western settlements and concessions in Shanghai to complete the takeover of this vital port city. Posters proclaimed the occupation of Shanghai by the Japanese Army in the name of His Imperial Majesty. World War II had caught up with the refugees again — this time at the other end of the Eurasian continent. The parading of the captured U.S. Marines through the streets of the city served as clear confirmation of the new situation that faced the refugees.

The fact that the yeshiva community and its allied groups of refugees were, after their long series of globe-spanning escapes, again prisoners of the Axis powers did not throw them into despair. With rare moral strength, derived from trust and faith in the Ruler of all events and His Heavenly protection, the refugees dedicated themselves to the ideal of still greater moral perfection. They saw the sole solution to their problems in intensification of their Torah studies.

As long as the Imperial Japanese forces were victoriously extending the boundaries of occupation deeper into the Asian mainland and across the vast Pacific Ocean, Shanghai remained isolated from the sounds of war, turning it into a tiny island of "peace," isolated by armies and navies from the rest of a warring world. This giant harbor of world trade, and the gateway to the Chinese continent, now found all of its land and sea lanes completely blocked. No person, no merchandise could enter the city; nor, by the same token, could any merchandise leave the city. And Shanghai possessed vast supplies of merchandise for world trade which were stored in its gigantic system of warehouses. This abundance in the midst of a world of scarcity was another remarkable phenomenon, another testament to the Divine concern for the welfare of the yeshiva community. There were, however, many months of famine through which the

Rabbi Abraham Kalmamowitz - the central power in all rescue efforts.

yeshiva community, along with the rest of the European refugees, had to struggle. This period of deprivation began with the outbreak of the Pacific war and prevailed among the stranded Jewish refugees until the outstanding effort and generosity of American charitable organizations improved their lot.

The yeshiva groups were basically supported by the famous Va'ad Hatzola organization, led by the untiring efforts of Rabbi Abraham Kalmanowitz and other great rabbis in the United States. Their indefatigable endeavors succeeded in raising the living standard of these groups while, by mutual agreement, the world-renowned American Jewish Joint Distribution Committee made its own effort to reach the general Jewish refugee population with the money they needed to buy supplies.

War Expanding to the Far East

Sustained by brotherly hands from across the sea, the refugee students and scholars immersed themselves even more deeply into the ocean of talmudic thought. Their absorption with Torah studies not only shut them off from the surrounding world but also enabled them to overcome nagging uncertainties about the fate of their loved ones. Delving into the depths of the Torah, they found respite from their fears and apprehensions concerning the lot of their people left behind in Europe.

At the outbreak of the Pacific war, Shanghai's Jewish refugees numbered about twenty thousand. There were basic differences in attitude and outlook between the yeshiva groups and many of the other eighteen thousand refugees — mostly from Austria and Germany — who had found a haven in Shanghai.

Jewish refugees selling their personal belongings to the Chinese population in Shanghai in order to buy food.

Operation: Torah Rescue

A large part of the refugees from Austria and Germany were living in the so-called "homes." These were barn-like buildings where privacy and living space for the individual were at a bare minimum.

The degrading living conditions and other depressing factors of poverty left their mark on the psyches of the refugees. They had no sense of the present tense in their lives. Their present existence, with its degradations and deprivations, was a complete vacuum in their existence. Whether standing in line for the meager portion of cooked food from the big kettles of the American Jewish Joint Distribution Committee or at their counterparts in front of

the local Jewish community kettle or in the cafe houses of Hongkew — the refugee ghetto quarter — their personal conversation was inevitably the same. It soon would turn to the better times of the individual's "glorious past," his position, his influence, and the power of his former wealth and possessions, enhancing his respectability and former lifestyle. His "now" had no value! It was not life, but mere existence. His "now" was swept under the carpet of his glorified past. Purposeless, it was no more than a necessary waiting period until he could realize his hopes and dreams of a better future.

By contrast the yeshiva community had no need to live in the fantasies of the past or in the hopes of the future. Its ability to function, create and develop was unaffected by the conditions in the refugees' lives. The Torah students needed no more than a *shtender* on which to place their books in order to find satisfaction and happiness in their continuous spiritual activities. In fact, their spiritual achievement had attained such a high level that some of the students even refused to utilize their precious American immigration visas, preferring to stay on in the intense atmosphere of Torah living, in spite of the suffering and the constant potential danger.

Operation: Torah Rescue

In remarkable contrast to the prevailing atmosphere of stress and tension - especially in the ghetto era - was the outstanding phenomenon of overflowing happiness and rejoicing at each of the weddings which took place during those years. An incredible outpouring of brotherly love, dedication, and identification with the joy of the bride and groom, demonstrating a closeness normally felt only for a genuine brother or sister, transformed such personal celebrations into family festivals that encompassed almost the entire Torah community. This sharing of one another's joys and sorrows on so intense a level was never again attained - even later, in the relaxed atmosphere of the most affluent celebrations in the United States, with joyous crowds filling luxurious wedding halls to capacity.

The Mashgiach officiates at wedding of Rabbi Shmuel Edeltuch.

At the reception for the chosson before the chuppah. Head table: (l. to r.) Rabbi Chayim Shmuelevitz, Mirrer Rosh Yeshiva; Rabbi Shimon Kalish, Amshenover Rebbe; the chosson, Rabbi Levi Fleishaker; Rabbi Meir Ashkenazi, Rav of Shanghai; Rabbi Yechezkel Levenstein, Mirrer Mashgiach

Esrogim in China

One of the perpetual problems in Jewish Diaspora life is the need to supply outlying Jewish communities with certain religious objects. Among the most difficult to provide is the *esrog*, one of the four plant species required for the Sukkos festival. The remaining three — palm branches, myrtles and willow tree branches — are easily procured, as they grow in standard shape in a variety of climates. However, Jewish people make a tremendous effort every year to obtain the special citrus fruit called an *esrog*, in order to fulfill a Divine commandment on the Sukkos holidays.

For several decades, the Jewish community of Shanghai received its *esrogim* through the effort of a pious Jewish family, the Abraham family, which eventually became one of the richest in the world, their name being synonymous with commerce and international trade. When the head of this Baghdad family had arrived in Shanghai — after having tried his fortune in Bombay — he brought along his wife and numerous children, and, among his few worldly possessions, a goat and an *esrog* plant. The goat provided the family with its own "Jewish" milk, while the *esrog* plant supplied the holiday fruits each year, after being replanted at the family's new home. It now also guaranteed a steady supply of *esrogim* for the yeshiva community, once the Sukkos holiday arrived.

But their joy lasted only until Pearl Harbor, when Mr. David Abraham and all the members of his family — being British subjects — were arrested by the Japanese together with all the citizens of the Allied countries. Eventually they were interned in a civilian prisoner-of-war camp to share the lot of all the British subjects and American citizens in Shanghai. Their properties were confiscated by the Imperial Japanese Army, and David Abraham's mansion and gardens in Shanghai were taken over by a Japanese admiral.

One result of this personal calamity of the Abraham family was that the Jews of Shanghai were deprived of their sole source for *esrogim*. As a last-ditch solution, someone dispatched a Chinese with orders to climb the tall walls surrounding the Abraham gardens and to pick some *esrogim*. True, the illustrious Imperial army was unable to foil this "coup," but in retaliation apparently decided to uproot the *esrog* tree, because shortly afterwards the news spread that the tree had been cut down. The Jews of Shanghai were now faced, for the first time in years, with the necessity of finding a new source of *esrogim*.

Before the approach of the following Sukkos festival, many plans were devised to provide Shanghai's Jewry with the *esrogim* essential for fulfilling the *mitzva*. There was a multitude of difficulties to overcome. The first stumbling block: how to translate, explain, or even hint to the Chinese the type of fruit that was sought. All the drawings of an *esrog* were to no avail. Finally, a delegation was formed which consisted of two refugees and a Chinese guide that went on an *esrog*-finding expedition into the hinterlands of China. According to some knowledgeable Chinese informants, there were certain regions where *esrog* trees were alleged to grow.

Operation: Torah Rescue

The findings of the expedition members were of questionable value, but their experiences were unique. Most of the population in the interior of China had never encountered any sort of white-skinned man before. Wherever the delegation arrived, it caused a sensation similar to a royal visit, with its attendant air of respect and honor. Many peasants they met attempted to touch their white skin and feel its texture.

At last the elusive Chinese *esrog* turned up, on a vacation site for wealthy Chinese businessmen, near the city of Hangchow. There, luxurious palaces had been built amidst beautiful gardens and artificial lakes and streamlets that were channeled under and around its edifices. In these surroundings, *esrog*-like fruits were discovered. But a problem arose: was this a genuine *esrog* fit for use as prescribed by Torah law? It had a strange extension growing out from the main fruit that bore a similarity to the fingers of a human hand. For that reason it was called in Chinese "God's hand."

The "explorers" brought back with them samples of their *esrog* for display. Many of the scholars were skeptical about the *esrog* they exhibited. Some experts in *halacha* used this *esrog* for the religious observance without pronouncing the customary blessing over it — to denote their doubts regarding its authenticity. Some merely used it for a symbolic commemoration and physical reminder of the *mitzva*. Others refused to use this fruit at all, insisting that it could not in any way be used as an *esrog* required by Jewish Law.

Japan and the "Final Solution"

As long as the Berlin-Tokyo Axis powers were still victorious, the Germans pressured their Japanese allies to fulfill the terms of their treaty for cultural cooperation. One of the implicit stipulations of that German treaty was the pursuit and genocide of the Jewish people, to annihilate the wretched survivors of German persecution no matter how far they had fled from their persecutors to territories under Japanese control.

When the venerable *Amshenover Rebbe* once traveled by railroad from Kobe to Tokyo, three German army officers who passed through his coach discovered "this Jew" among his Japanese co-travelers. The sight of a archetypal Jew with his long, white beard and sidelocks, dressed in traditional Chassidic garb, infuriated the pure-blooded Aryans. They yelled and cursed in their anger at finding a Jew, destined for extermination, who had escaped to that far-away corner of the world. Venting their hate-filled madness, they screamed, "The Gestapo has long arms. You dirty Jews think you can escape German power? Even if you flee to the very end of the world, we will reach and destroy you." They struck and kicked the helpless old man in front of the shocked Japanese while he attempted to protect his face and body with his hands and heavy coat.

(l. to r.) Rabbi Sholom Shapiro, Prof. Abraham Kotsuji, Rabbi Shimon Kalish (Amshenover Rebbe), Rabbi Shatskes (Lomzer Rav), Capt. Fukamachi, Leo Hanin

Ghetto guarantee required by Japanese authorities for registration of "stateless refugees". Signature at lower right is that of Rabbi Boruch Borchardt – a prime organizer and influential leader of Agudath Israel movement in America.

Mutual Guarantee and Mutual Responsibility Bond

We, the undersigned, are willing to guarantee that the persons mentioned overleaf in this form are bona fide residents and will never ~~permit any hostile acts~~

In the event of violation of their respective pledges of good conduct, the undersigned will accept full responsibility.

Signature: sgd. Jacob Gilmovicz   sgd. B. Borchardt
Address:- 17 ......   304/5 ......
Date: 13-7-42

Japan and the Final Solution

Then, abruptly, the Germans turned from their victim and proceeded to the next car.

Germany was not satisfied with the mere display of a giant-size anti-Semitic caricature of a Jew on an outside wall of a Tokyo department store, or with anti-Semitic press campaigns. And so, the Germans took concrete steps to annihilate the Jews who were fortunate enough to have escaped to the ends of the globe.

A German submarine brought two Nazis to Japanese-occupied Singapore to instruct and guide the Japanese in the German system of ghettoes and concentration and extermination camps. A rumor had it that one of the Nazis aboard the submarine was the infamous German Gestapo chieftain, Josef Meisinger, "the Butcher of Warsaw," who as Warsaw's Gestapo commander in 1939 had murdered tens of thousands of Jews.

A proclamation posted by the Imperial Japanese Army headquarters all over the city of Shanghai hit the population with lightning surprise. The district of Hongkew, a bombed-out slum area around the harbor, and the nearby munition plants had been designated as a ghetto for Jews. All the Jews who had escaped to Shanghai from persecution in Europe were now declared "stateless refugees." They were forced to abandon their homes and were only allowed to take the most essential belongings to their new shelters within the assigned Chinese slum area. Any stateless refugee found outside the ghetto area without special permission after May 18, 1943, would be subject to severe penalty.

The idea of exterminating an entire people was alien to the Japanese; the German concept of the "International Jew," was also unknown to this Asian nation. Many efforts were initiated to exempt various Jewish groups from the Imperial edict. These efforts were directed at winning the good will of certain Japanese officials connected with the ghetto decree. Vast sums of money were spent on these attempts to buy exemptions. Nevertheless, the bulk of the Jewish refugee population of Shanghai had to start the trek to the ghetto.

During the two years after the initial institution of the ghetto system, rumors spread from time to time about new "administrative decrees" to confine the already overcrowded ghetto to increasingly smaller areas. Each of such changes would have meant additional suffering through resettlement within an already intolerably overcrowded living space. But oddly, each time such a rumor about an impending decree was leaked, it was hotly denied by the Japanese, who branded it "enemy propaganda" to smear the good name of Japan.

Many rumors circulated among the refugees. The most persistent was that the infamous Josef Meisinger was exerting active pressure on the Japanese to deal with "their" Jews "decisively" — in accordance with the German "final solution" of the "Jewish problem."

For shocking revelations about one "final solution" planned for the Jews of Shanghai even before the establishment of the ghetto, see the book *Or Yechezkel*,* the published letters of the *mashgiach* of Mirrer Yeshiva, Rabbi Yechezkel Levenstein. For more details also see *The Fugu Plan*, or *Desperate Voyagers*.**

These books reveal the steps that were outlined by the notorious mass murderer of close to one hundred thousand Jews of Warsaw, Gestapo Colonel Josef Meisinger. In the decisive top secret meeting for the liquidation of

---

* Rabbi Yechezkel Levenstein, *Or Yechezkel* (Bnei Brak: Yeshivat Ponevez, 1976), 355-56.
** Marvin Tokayer and Mary Swartz, *The Fugu Plan* (London-New York: Paddington Press Ltd., 1979),

Shanghai's Jews, with the participation of representatives of the Japanese army and navy including Tsutomu Kubota, the director of the Office for Refugee Affairs and later ghetto chief, representatives of the Japanese consulate and the chief of the German Information Bureau, Meisinger created the atmosphere and spirit for Japanese participation in the liquidation of the Jews. Supported by a display of pictures, maps and detailed material, he proposed to the Japanese, among various alternatives for the destruction of the common Jewish enemy, to announce to Shanghai's Jews their relocation to a safer island for their protection against eventual American bombardments. The ships which would transport them to the island would "sink" on the high seas, solving the Jewish problem for the Japanese. Later it would be covered up by reporting an accident and the sighting of shipwrecks at sea.

This proposition to drown all Jews on the high seas after leading them onto unseaworthy boats was accepted. For compliance with the German solution of the "Jewish problem," the local Japanese power structure was offered a fat reward: Self-enrichment from the tremendous spoils of Shanghai's total Jewish population. This included the properties, businesses and mansions of rich Russian Jews, and Sephardic Jews who had Iraqi citizenship and were therefore not interned as subjects of the British Empire. The top-secret plan had to be executed within two weeks, when all Jews could be rounded up at once in their synagogues on the Rosh Hashana holiday.

But, as the citation goes in Rabbi Yechezkel Levenstcin's book: Behold the Guardian of Israel neither slumbers nor sleeps.... The foolproof plan leaked out as a result of the strange thoughts that tormented one of the participants of the fateful meeting, Mitsugi Shibata, a vice-consul at Japan's Shanghai consulate. He knew well that such detailed plans of the local army and navy leadership would not be interfered with by even the highest authorities in Tokyo. He also knew that he would risk his own life by revealing those irrevocable measures. Still, Shibata could not silence his conscience, especially if such a massacre were carried out and he had not divulged to some Jewish friend the awful plans for the Jews' annihilation. Under the force of his guilt, he leaked the secret to his Jewish friends. These community leaders put together the amount of half a million U.S. dollars to bribe the Japanese commanders with this "donation for the Japanese war widows and orphans."

The Japanese were stunned and furious that this secret had leaked out and under gruesome torture they extracted from the arrested leaders of the community the identity of the "traitor," the source of their information. The vice consul, who attended a special meeting at the residence of their community leader Michael Speelman, and seven Jewish leaders were arrested and almost beaten to death in the notorious Bridge House prison. It was a miracle that after weeks of cruel torture they came out alive. No wonder that they all heeded the stern warning of the Japanese not to talk about their experience. Only after the war did they reveal their secret.

However, in order not to blemish Japanese history with the stain of their share in the barbaric extermination of the Jews, the entire undertaking was immediately called off and Shanghai's Jews were saved from annihilation.

There were other instances where plans for the Jews' annihilation miraculously were called off. At one point, an ominous sign of evil developments for the hapless refugees was a proclamation suddenly posted in public places within the ghetto, ordering "stateless persons" — a synonym for Jews — to pack their possessions in orderly fashion, with detailed lists of their belongings attached to it. These lists were to be kept with the luggage keys so as to have them ready to hand over to the authorities upon relocation. It was being planned in order to give every Jew an opportunity for "useful occupation" and work. (This was the ruse the Germans used for deportation of Jews to the death camps.) These posters were removed after a few days without any official explanation. The refugees speculated that policy wrangles among powerful factions within the Kem Peitai — the ultimate secret power structure of the Japanese occupation bureaucracy — were responsible for the sudden changes of policy.

Many of the refugees saw this reversal as one more manifestation of the protecting hand of Heavenly Providence. In Europe, the very same plans were being carried out to the bitter end! But in China the refugee community, with the groups of Torah scholars among them, would remain alive in spite of all the threats of death and doom.

Law and Punishment the Japanese Way

The more than two years of ghetto imprisonment were a time of constant apprehension for many individuals. The slightest transgression of ghetto regulations was met with severe and cruel punishment, for besides the sadistic instincts of the Japanese ghetto chiefs, there was also a deeply felt hatred for all "whites." In addition, the Japanese took an overbearing pride in the sanctity of every Imperial decree.

In contrast, however, an incident which involved the yeshiva group as a whole was treated with uncharacteristic leniency. Some Mirrer Yeshiva students rebelled against the planned ghetto internment. They found it especially demeaning that they would be lodged in a Salvation Army building, together with the scum of Shanghai — its drunks, ex-convicts and other derelicts. They carried their protest to the offices of SACRA — Shanghai Askenazi Collaborating Relief Association — the Japanese-appointed Jewish ghetto administrative council. Some office equipment and pieces of furniture were damaged in this encounter.

According to Japanese tradition, every Japanese soldier or official is an executor of the emperor's will. To obstruct or defy that will invites instant punishment, even death. In

Japanese eyes, therefore, this incident was tantamount to a revolt against Japanese authority and would normally have resulted in cruel suffering and death for the group as a whole! Miraculously though, even those directly involved escaped punishment—all they received was a tongue-lashing. According to experts on Japanese psychology, this behavior was nothing short of an open miracle.

To understand the unusualness of this leniency, perhaps it is useful to repeat a story that is told about a certain bridge which was guarded by a Japanese soldier against sabotage. All Japanese and Chinese crossing the bridge were required to bow down to this soldier in his role as representative of His Imperial Majesty. Even "whites" had to tip their hats to him. At the end of an exhausting workday, an absent-minded Chinese coolie with a heavy load on his shoulder forgot to pay this respect to the soldier-guard; he was decapitated immediately by the watchful soldier with his saber.

Only the strenuous effort of the newly-created SACRA (Judenrat), using all kinds of excuses and influences to minimize the "insult" to Japanese Imperial power, prevented the severest punishment from being meted out to the yeshiva students. Surprisingly, the students' "revolt," in spite of its confrontational character, did not provoke the Japanese to stern insistence on their decree. The demonstrators were most happy to receive assurances that no one of the Torah students would be forced into the Salvation Army compound.

Incidentally, the above mentioned warehouse of the Salvation Army was completely leveled at a later date during an air raid by the American air force.

The Power of Intensive Torah Study

The story of the Shanghai ghetto would be incomplete without mentioning some more details of the unexpected and unexplainable preferential treatment accorded to the yeshiva students.

The one characteristic that marked all the ghetto laws and decrees was the humiliation and degradation that they inflicted on the unfortunate victims. For a large segment of the refugee population, imprisonment within the ghetto area meant being cut off from even the meager earnings they had formerly had from occasional odd jobs performed in the city outside the ghetto walls. The opportunity to maintain a minimum standard of living was now wiped out by the ghetto decree.

Although the Japanese issued permits to leave the ghetto for gainful outside employment, to obtain such a "ghetto pass," one was required to show steady employment guaranteed by the employer. For many of these occasional jobs, such proof could not be furnished. In addition, applicants for passes had to wait in line for hours under a burning sun and, when their turn finally came, were subjected to insulting and cruel interrogations by the ghetto chiefs. The interrogation usually included being yelled at and called all kinds of degrading epithets.

The Power of Intensive Torah Study

At right:
Rabbi Yehoshua Godlefsky, studying Talmud in Museum Road Synagogue. He later became founder and director of Keren Hayeled Rescue Fund in Eretz Yisrael.

Below:
Study group: (r. to l.) Rabbis Avrohom Arbus, Moshe Bunim Pirotinsky, Nochum Lesman, Shmuel Birnbaum, Shalom Shapiro, Nochum Perzovitz, Jacob Finkelstein, Zvi Kahane, Avrohom Dovid Niznik, Aron Kreiser, Moshe Leizersohn

Often, applicants were beaten or slapped in the face because the interrogator always "knew better" and punished the poor applicants for being "damned liars." Since ghetto passes were granted for only short periods of time (the so-called "seasonal" pass, the longest available term, was valid only for three months) every extension or renewal was a trauma for the applicant, since it meant exposing himself to the whims and sadism of the two Japanese ghetto chiefs who issued the passes.

Punishment for any failure to comply exactly with the terms of the pass — its time of departure and return or the route to be followed when traveling between the ghetto and the place of employment — often had fatal consequences. Even one day in the notorious Ward Road jail could be a death sentence. The cells were infested with lice that carried an incurable type of deadly typhus bacillus.

Braving the climate of harassment and persecution that permeated Jewish life under the ghetto decrees, the yeshiva community dedicated itself more than ever to its studies. With unbending perseverance, the scholars pursued their studies day and night. During daytime hours they studied in the Beis Aharon or Museum Road Synagogue located in the very center of the former International Settlement, outside the ghetto area. Many continued studying even after returning to the ghetto — before the nightly 11 P.M. curfew — in the special Night Yeshiva Center that was opened for this purpose in the ghetto.

Even under the new conditions, the yeshiva element escaped the worst of the ordeals and torment. The rules and regulations regarding these students contradicted the spirit of the ghetto laws and stood in startling contrast to Japanese conduct toward the vast majority of ghetto inmates.

The Power of Intensive Torah Study

Ghetto pass of the author

Operation: Torah Rescue

By order of the authorities, all residents of the Shanghai ghetto were required to wear this badge whenever leaving the ghetto area.

Initially, the students were collectively presented with yeshiva group-passes for leaving and reentering the ghetto in groups, thus allowing them to continue their studies even outside the ghetto confines. Later, unbelievably, every student was presented with his own pass, delivered in person by a high-ranking Japanese official of the ghetto administration who appeared in the office of the yeshiva for this purpose. This was quite a contrast to the humiliating official routine that the other ghetto inhabitants were forced to endure while standing for hours in line under a burning subtropical sun to obtain a pass. It was just one more demonstration of the persistent and extraordinary Heavenly guidance for the Torah camp.

Through all these persecutions and ghetto decrees, the community of yeshiva scholars braved the pressures and dangers by deeply immersing themselves in their hallowed studies. They excluded all outside interests and thoughts of personal comfort for the sake of attaining greater perfection in their religious endeavors. In the pursuit of these lofty goals, they were granted extraordinary privileges under continuous Divine protection.

Traces of Idolatry in the Twentieth Century

One of the puzzling phenomena to the Western observer was the Japanese belief in the godliness of His Imperial Majesty, the Emperor — at least until as recently as VA (Victory in Asia) Day.

Foreigners were aware that the Japanese, walking past the entrance to the emperor's palace, had to bow in the direction of the inner royal court. Unknown to most observers, this was not merely a sign of respect for a mortal emperor; it also constituted an act of religious worship. The emperor was regarded as a god, who descended directly from the "Almighty Father," the sun — whose son, cast down to earth, landed safely, a first man on a Japanese island. The emperor, therefore a descendant of this "son," was treated as a god by all his subjects. When His Majesty was ill, the consulting physician was not permitted to touch the emperor's body with his bare fingers; he had to wear special fine silk gloves for the examination.

The rising sun on the Japanese flag is not a mere decorative design. It is symbolic of Japanese life and beliefs. The emperor, descendant of the sun-god, was also believed to be the father of the entire Japanese nation. The Japanese people multiplied, raising and preserving

Operation: Torah Rescue

the ideal of "one family," with their emperors being the godly fathers of this one family ideal that survived to the present day.

This one family concept explained the devotion of each Japanese to his emperor, the "family head" of the nation. If in wartime a soldier could not hold the position assigned to him, he would not disappoint the emperor, the head of the Japanese family, and abandon his assignment. He would defend his position to the very end and then finish his life by hara-kiri — disemboweling himself with a sword for failing to carry out the mission entrusted to him. Being killed in action was a perfect way of ending one's life and of fulfilling one's duty in faithfulness to the Japanese people and to its divine emperor. The warrior's soul would then continue to live as a star in heaven with all the other souls of Japanese heroes and warriors, the samurai of all times.

The Westerner was struck with amazement and disbelief upon witnessing a mother run joyfully to all her neighbors, waving a letter from the army with the wonderful news that her son had offered himself as the ultimate sacrifice for the emperor and the nation.

The climax of all these strange beliefs, however, came near the end of the war, when the Japanese advance was halted in Burma and in the Indonesian Islands near Australia. When the fortunes of war had turned against Japan and one island after the other was lost — as defeat followed defeat — the Japanese belief in idolatry, especially in their biggest god, the sun, played a major role in strengthening the nation's morale.

One morning, the most reputable English-language newspaper, *The Shanghai Times*, came out with banner headlines:

Traces of Idolatry in the Twentieth Century

EMPEROR HAS INTERVIEW WITH GRANDFATHER!

It was reported that His Imperial Highness, the Emperor, is going to meet with his grandfather — the Sun — in a certain shrine, to discuss with him the war situation and plan effective means against the advancing Americans.

From the ordinary man in the street to the intellectual, there were exchanges of greetings and congratulations. A new spirit replaced the air of gloom that had pervaded the hearts and minds of the Japanese people.

Could an outsider resist wondering about such incredible idolatrous naiveté, on the part of the most modern and technologically advanced nation in Asia? Surely, one needed all of his self-control in order to maintain an air of seriousness after hearing the fantastic report of the sun and the emperor meeting. A truly most startling discovery: ancient idolatry had still found an outlet, in the midst of the twentieth century!

The Last Battles of World War II

During 1943 and 1944, the fortunes of war turned increasingly against Japan. With the Japanese fleet defeated, the United States Navy leapfrogged from island to island, liberating vast areas of the Pacific from Japanese rule. Powerful and well-fortified islands could not withstand the onslaught of American military might, despite all the desperation and heroism displayed by its Japanese defenders. It was only a question of time before the home islands of Japan proper would be invaded.

Under the circumstances, the position of Shanghai became increasingly precarious. It was feared that a direct attack on Japan would cost the Americans immense loss of life and material. It was therefore imperative to open a second front on the Chinese mainland as a base to support an attack on Japan proper. Such a second front would be a deadly threat to the rear of the Japanese armies on the Asian continent.

Knowing that Shanghai was of prime importance to the enemy, the Japanese High Command made elaborate preparations to fortify the city and resolved to turn it, if necessary, into a second Stalingrad. Of course, all the determination and effort on both sides to control this key port on the Chinese mainland spelled great danger to the civilian population and for the survival of the unique groups of Jewish refugees stranded here.

The first phase of the Allied drive to capture Shanghai saw a sharp increase of steady American air raids. Night after night, at precisely the same hour and almost to the minute, the air raid sirens would warn the population to take shelter. The targets were the military plants around the port and its naval installations which the Japanese had placed close by or within the Jewish ghetto settlements. To bolster the Japanese military installations, the helpless refugees were thus positioned as targets for American bombardments in the hope that the Americans would not bomb the civilian refugee population.

After the Japanese air defenses were sufficiently crippled, the air raids were extended into the daylight hours. Many war scenes remain indelibly inscribed in the memories of the participants: the omnipresent tension of imminent death and destruction under air bombardments; synagogues which became impromptu places of refuge for miracle-seeking worshipers; the many people crowded closely together and hitting the floor of the packed sanctuary when the bombs exploded; mothers hovering over their children, shielding them with their own bodies from shell fragments. Almost continuous were the unforgettable sounds of Psalms and prayers recited in unison during the bombardments, drowned out by the ear-shattering shrieks of exploding bombs, and the roar of airplanes flying overhead.

Many survived the devastating air bombardments by sheer miracle. One yeshiva student was taking an afternoon nap on his bed when the air raid alarm was sounded. His house was hit during the bombardment. The young man, together with the bed and the floor and walls of his room, fell to the street where he was buried under the ruins and rubble of the bombed-out house — in complete darkness, with but a single, faraway ray of light showing in the distance. When he finally managed to free himself from under the pile of debris to reach daylight, he ran in shock, half-dazed and barely conscious of what had happened, into a nearby house. In a mirror, he discovered himself to be covered beyond recognition with dust and dirt, his face completely blackened by the soot of the pulverized particles of his former house, yet miraculously unhurt.

Even as the air raids continued, the Japanese concentrated their planning on an all out defense of Shanghai. Main streets and important thoroughfares and intersections were turned into fortified positions protected by high barriers of sandbags. Tall buildings, their foundations fortified and protected with sandbag walls, were converted for use as anti-aircraft, artillery, or machine-gun positions. On the main streets, sidewalks were dug up for foxholes at every few yards, to be manned by Japanese soldiers. This capital of commerce and world trade was systematically being converted into a veritable fortress. The Japanese boasted that they would turn Shanghai into a second Stalingrad and would never permit this vital seaport to fall into the enemies' hands intact.

The thorough preparations were an indication to the civilian population of what they could expect in the future. In addition, they were aware of the recent history of Manila, the capital of the Japanese-occupied Philippines. It revealed to Shanghai's civilian population what terrible fate might befall them. There too, the Japanese had vowed not to surrender the city. They defended each city block from their mini-fortresses and foxhole positions, determined to destroy as many of the enemy as possible before dying in their holes, either at the hand of the

The Last Battles of World War II

enemy or by committing hara-kiri, the form of suicide the Japanese considered an honorable option preferable to surrendering to the enemy. With this resolve, Manila was defended until it was set afire. When it became clear that the city would be overrun by the American forces, the Japanese decided to deprive the enemy of the fruits of his victory. During the final days of their suicidal resistance, the Japanese troops went on a rampage, killing all their supposed enemies among Manila's civilian population. No wonder the battle preparations in the streets of Shanghai had such a depressing effect on the white inhabitants of Shanghai, who recognized their helplessness in the event of a savage fight for the city and the even more barbarous consequences should the Japanese face defeat.

Despite the ever-increasing preparations for a decisive battle, the Torah community and its leaders were constantly on the alert for finding ways of rescue. There was a plan by one group, seeking an escape route toward the north, to the city of Tientsin. But the leadership of the largest group, the Mirrer yeshiva, did not want to chance the dangers of an overland trek to the north, fearing possible attacks from savage tribesmen and mobs of natives in an unknown Chinese hinterland.

In those days of deliberations, weighing the risks of action versus inaction, the lot of the Gaon of Vilna was again cast — just like at previous crossroads of life and death. The pages of a Bible were again consulted by the same distinguished member of the community. Once more, the response seemed miraculously decisive to the famous questioner.

The scriptural verse that was ultimately indicated was in the Book of Isaiah (37:35):*And I will bestow My protection upon this city, and I will save it* (from the wrath of the king of Assyria), *for the sake of My Name and for the sake of My servant David.* The implicit parallels to the situation were obvious

From the winter of 1945, the students learned for nine months in an old warehouse on Baikel Road. Although weak and sagging, the structure somehow withstood the heavy bombings in the month of Av, while the Mashgiach and the entire student body recited Tehillim fervently. In Elul, after the Japanese surrender, they moved to another building. One day a group of students went for a walk and later reported the startling news that the building on Baikel Road was a shambles. It had apparently collapsed, some time after the Yeshiva had safely abandoned it.

and striking. It resolved the problems of the situation clearly.

"I will bestow My protection upon this city," in this situation, clearly referred to Shanghai and directly addressed the problem of survival in the strategic city. "I will save it (from the wrath of the king of Assyria)" referred to the devastating effect of any American attack against the city. "For the sake of My Name and for the sake of My servant David" related to the yeshiva community and their concentration on the service and worship of the Almighty at all times. Thus, the verse gave assurance of survival to the city for the sake of its inhabitants, God's devoted servants, allegorically represented by King David.

The debates, the problems, the doubts, and the risks — all the uncertainties of an attempted escape from Shanghai — were suddenly resolved and put to rest. It was decided to stay on in the beleaguered city in expectation of God's mercy. None of the scholars had any knowledge at that time of the development of the atomic bomb by the United States government. No one could imagine how quickly the Pacific War would come to an end and all of Shanghai's feverish preparations for battle would prove unnecessary.

33
Efforts to Save Torah Scholars

While the transformation of Shanghai into a fortified city went on at great speed, no efforts were spared on the other side of the Pacific in an all-out humanitarian endeavor to save the stranded refugee scholars from the approaching inferno. Under the leadership of the untiring and self-sacrificing humanitarian, the venerable and renowned Rabbi Abraham Kalmanowitz, every attempt was made to coordinate various rescue undertakings. Rabbi Kalmanowitz approached the Department of State, the Pope, the Soviet government and the king of Sweden as parties who could be instrumental in rescuing the community of refugees from Shanghai.

Russia flatly refused to cooperate, explaining that the Trans-Siberian Railroad system could not transport such a large group of refugees back to Europe, specifically to Sweden, as it was already overloaded with military transports. This answer sounded insensitive to observers at the time, since the Russian front lines were thousands of miles from Siberia and were moving deeper into Europe. But the subsequent Russian entry on a massive scale into Manchuria and other vital areas of the Asian continent — after the Japanese defeat — gave a degree of justification to Russia's refusal.

The king of Sweden, Gustav V, on the other hand, was not satisfied just to offer his land as a haven to the faraway refugees. In the spirit of a great and truly noble monarch, he also instructed his royal consulate in Shanghai to "spare no effort" and to transform the area surrounding the consulate into a veritable "island of refuge" should the flames of war engulf the city. At His Majesty's orders, houses were bought within several blocks of the consulate and the Swedish flag raised over them. The royal Swedish emblem was painted on the roofs and walls to show airplanes and infantry alike that these houses enjoyed the sanctity of neutrality as extensions of Sweden's consular territory. According to the plan of this great Swedish humanitarian, the houses of the Swedish compound were to be opened solely to refugees if the battle should reach the confines of the city. Till then, the purpose of this complex undertaking was to be kept confidential; only a few communal leaders were let in on the secret.

The final, frightful stage of scrambling to reach this modern Noah's ark—in a scenario of desperation and panic when crossing the fires of battle to escape an inferno of death and destruction—never materialized. The dropping of the atom bomb on Hiroshima was the shocking and unforgettable historic event that saved the lives of some of the world's future Jewish leaders.

When the news of Japan's final surrender hit the city, the scenes of joy were almost indescribable. In the midst of feverish preparations for battle that promised tremendous civilian suffering and destruction, the news of deliverance and peace were the sudden end to a nightmare! Was it a pure coincidence of numbers that the tragedy of the A-bomb that initially killed 20,000 at Hiroshima saved 20,000 refugees in their ghetto and spared many more from incalculable misery?

So complete and radical was the sudden reversal of the

Operation: Torah Rescue

Mr. Ghoya, former chief and self-styled "king" of Shanghai ghetto, after Japanese surrender

fears and tensions at the news of Japan's surrender, that many burst into tears of joy. Others broke into singing the traditional *Hallel*, psalms of thanksgiving to the Supreme Governor of human destiny. Families and friends kissed one another and fell into each other's arms in the overwhelming happiness of being saved from death and endless suffering. But few realized that it was the most destructive period in the history of the Jewish people that had just come to an end.

In Review

The remnants of Torah scholarship, driven by the force of events to the far end of the Eurasian continent, were exposed to the horrors of World War II from the very beginning in Europe to its dramatic end in Asia, many months after VE (Victory in Europe) Day. But their story, with its astounding series of miraculous rescues, was the exact opposite of the appalling fate of the bulk of European Jewry. It seemed that the Heavenly grace denied to the Jewish masses of Europe, was being showered in its full, startling abundance upon this group of Torah refugees.

Only when the outer limits of the Jewish settlement in Europe were reached did the power of the German armies suddenly weaken and their advance abruptly come to a standstill. A destiny seemed to have been fulfilled, and the conquest therefore came to an end. At Stalingrad and the approaches to the Caucasian mountains, the drive of this formidable German war machine turned powerless and started a sudden reversal, as if some secret goal had been reached.

In analyzing the military campaigns in the European war theater, their movements and their repercussions on the fate of the Jewish people, one must also reevaluate certain aspects of two hundred years of modern Jewish history. Jewish assimilation within the nations of the Diaspora started with the Reform movement in Germany, spread to Austria and Hungary, later to Eastern Europe, and finally to Russia. It was the most striking mass abandonment of Torah culture and life-style in Jewish history.

The ultimate result of the Jewish Reform movement was the devastating assimilation it fostered, and the great number of interfaith marriages that spelled an abrupt end for the chain of Jewish generations. Population figures for the Jews in Germany when the Nazis took power show only half a million Jews, while two-and-a-half million counted themselves as converted Jews whose grandfather, father, or they themselves had left the Jewish fold to embrace the religions of their environment.

The conquering German armies and the ensuing Jewish suffering followed the very same path as the assimilation. They started in Germany, spreading to Austria, Eastern Europe, and finally they came to an end upon reaching the last outskirts of Russia's Jewish settlements — Leningrad, Stalingrad and the foot of the Caucasian mountains. There the formidable German war machine suddenly lost its drive and power.

In this context, another quite remarkable feature should be mentioned: the startling German theory of racism — of the superiority of the blue-eyed, blond-haired Aryans — that became law in Germany. It contended that even if someone's father or grandfather was a Jew who had converted to Christianity, the second and even the third generation Christians were still to be considered Jews and subject to the German laws against Jews. Converted Jews, who had considered themselves Christians and "secure" in the lap of the Church, were driven to despair and suicide.

The entire theory of Aryanism was completely

unscientific, especially in view of the total mingling of all kinds of races, nations and groups within the international fabric of modern social life. The rest of the world found it incomprehensible that an educated, scientific nation such as the Germans would embrace such pseudoscientific fantasies. Yet all these strange phenomena fulfilled the Biblical testimony of God's oath that should His people say, "Let us become like all the nations...I shall (assert My) rule over you with a strong hand, and outstretched arm and with outpoured fury" (Ezekiel 20:32-33).

35

In Perspective: The Fuehrer and the Anti-Fuehrer

When analyzing the rise to power of the two leading political figures of World War II, one whose power led to its outbreak and the other whose power led to its termination, we discern several parallel elements. Furthermore, their ascendance to power was accompanied by a number of most unusual and baffling developments.

Why should Hitler's second attempt to grab power in Germany in 1933 have been more acceptable to the Germans than his first coup d'etat—the "Munich *Putsch*"—attempted after the catastrophic German inflation and depression of 1921 to 1923? How could an uneducated individual like Hitler have gained the leadership of the most advanced nation in science and technology in Europe? How could a house painter have become "Der Fuehrer," the leader of scientists, philosophers, thinkers, poets, and writers—when there couldn't be any wider gap separating a man from the people?

Just ten days before Hitler came to power, his opponent—and "antidote"—in the drama soon to unfold was inaugurated for his first term as president. This leader of the American people, Franklin D. Roosevelt, became the only man able to stop and reverse Hitler's victorious war

In Perspective: The Fuehrer and the Anti-Fuehrer

chariot. FDR kept rearming an already defeated Russia with a constant flow of the most modern weapons and enabled it to marshal new resistance against the Germans to eventually stop and reverse the German march toward world conquest.

Who was this powerful man who transformed his country and its industrial potential into a veritable arsenal for a defeated Europe and a beaten England? He was an individual one would have expected to be the most unsuitable for such a gigantic task. Seriously handicapped by polio, his advance to political power was accompanied by propaganda that showed him "already able" to sit up or even to stand in order to prove his vitality and physical ability. An invisible hand seemingly lifted him above his limitations to leadership of the world's potentially most powerful nation.

A person impeded by disability and preoccupied with the problems of his illness is usually distracted from the problems of his fellow men. Yet, in spite of all his own difficulties, this new president of the United States managed to cope with the staggering problems of a nation in the grip of a paralyzing economic depression. He generated unbelievable energy and vigor, and pulled the country out of the Great Depression. He innovated completely new systems for economic development with seemingly endless resourcefulness and genius.

Additionally, this handicapped man undertook and achieved a complete reversal of the psychology of his nation — an America that regretted its tremendous sacrifices in lives and money to salvage Europe in World War I only to be repaid with ingratitude! "Never again will we sacrifice a healthy America for a sick Europe," was the slogan. Gradually FDR got his country involved in saving the world from the German threat of world conquest and domination. He transformed his unarmed country into the world's most formidable weapons arsenal until the enemy was finally defeated.

This ill man, raised by Providence to become the antidote for the German aggressor, was put in power for his mission, a presidency, that started ten days before Hitler's power grab in Germany and ended abruptly with FDR's sickness and sudden death just before the doomed German beast was felled. His power and activity were the miraculous gifts required for the fulfillment of his mission in this world. They came to a sudden end when his task was fulfilled and his mission had been accomplished.

Fulfillment

The final chapter of Heavenly rescue for the Torah scholar survivors was written in America. Similar to the repatriation of the so-called "displaced persons" in Europe, the transplantation of the Torah refugees from Shanghai to the United States and Israel took many months and various routes of migration.

The bulk of the refugees arrived in San Francisco, on America's West Coast, by ship during a period of several months. The Va'ad Hatzala and the Jewish community made arrangements for their stay and later transportation to New York.

Others followed the Mirrer *rosh hayeshiva*, Rabbi Chayim Shmuelevitz, to France with the intention of settling in Israel. Later this group split up and some decided to rejoin Mirrer Yeshiva in the United States.

However, not everybody was patient enough to wait his turn in leaving China. A few found their own means of transportation and documents to undertake the journey to the destination of their hearts — Palestine, through the Pacific and Indian Oceans and the Suez Canal. On their way, this group was arrested and put into an Egyptian jail for "lack of sufficient travel documents." They were freed through some intervention initiated in Jerusalem, and

Operation: Torah Rescue

finally were brought to Israel. In those days of mass migration of "displaced persons" after World War II, such forced "hospitality" in jails was quite common. Even some of those who made their way directly to the U.S. via the Pacific Ocean had their visas or travel papers challenged once they arrived in San Francisco. Students were forcibly held in detention, to be returned to China. But eventually they were admitted to the United States thanks to Rabbi Abraham Kalmanowitz's intervention with government authorities.

A sizable number of students were admitted to Canada. However, after months of effort, their plans to settle and create an influential center of Jewish studies did not materialize and this group eventually rejoined the Mirrer Yeshiva in the United States.

Rabbi Abraham Kalmanowitz thanking Henry Morgenthau, Jr. for assistance in rescue work. (L. to r.) Rabbi Alex Weisfogel, assistant to Rabbi Kalmanowitz; Rabbi Berman of Arverne, N.Y.; U.S. Secretary of the Treasury Henry Morgenthau; Rabbis Kalmanowitz, Levi Fleishaker, and Ben Zion Leitner.

When the main body of the Yeshiva's students and refugee scholars were finally reunited in New York, the city of New York accorded Mirrer Yeshiva an official welcome, including the presentation of the "Key to the City," an honor bestowed on only a few outstanding dignitaries and world leaders.

At this stage of resettlement, when the various groups of Torah refugees had rejoined the community of world Jewry, they met a Jewish nation mourning the greatest tragedy in its sorrow- and grief-filled history.

European Jewry, the wellspring of Torah and Jewish scholarship, filled with aspirations and creativity — the very heart and lifeblood of the Jewish people — was decimated. Only a few tattered individuals survived the deluge of hatred and murder that had swept their communities,

After arrival in U.S.: (l. to r.) Rabbi Nochum Perzovitz, later Mirrer Rosh Yeshiva, Jerusalem; Rabbi Moshe Bernstein, Kamenitzer Rosh Yeshiva, Jerusalem; Rabbi Sholom Menashe Gotlieb, Rosh Yeshiva of Beth Hatalmud, Brooklyn, NY; Rabbi Osher Lichtstein, later Kamenitzer Rosh Yeshiva, Jerusalem

Operation: Torah Rescue

which temporarily had been denied the Heavenly protection that had guided them through the millennia of exile.

In this time of mourning and despair, the yeshiva scholars, the standard-bearers of the nation, fortified by the chain of unending miracles that had provided their own deliverance, decided to fulfill their Heavenly mission to rebuild Torah and Jewry. These survivors of the most devastating war, to which they were exposed from its first moment in Poland to its last phase on VJ (Victory in Japan) Day in Asia, considered themselves to have been saved for the purpose of carrying over the eternal flame of the Torah heritage. Their yeshiva, like the Yavneh of ancient Israel, was the spark of reconstruction that made possible the rebuilding of Torah scholarship for the Jewish people and guaranteed its survival through the continuation of the chain of Jewish learning.

Mirrer Yeshiva on three continents – before and after the Holocaust: (above left) in Mir, Poland; (left) in Jerusalem; (below) in Brooklyn

The scholars threw themselves wholeheartedly into the struggle to reconstruct Jewish communal life through founding and building Torah schools, particularly institutions of higher Jewish studies. As teachers and leaders, instructors and organizers in America, in Israel and many other countries, they led a spectacular revival of the Jewish nation, and of a new American-born generation dedicated to the ideals of Torah life.

The resurrection of the Mirrer Yeshiva, both in Israel and America, the reestablishment of numerous former institutions, and the founding of many new schools of Jewish and talmudic studies were initiated. These contributed to the renaissance of Torah life among all groups in the American Diaspora. In addition, the already existing American yeshivos, famous institutes like the yeshivos of Telshe, Kamenitz and Novardok, and numerous Chassidic yeshivos, were even if only indirectly stimulated by their influence. New networks of education for girls were founded, and the expansion of existing schools under the names of Bais Yaakov, Bais Rivka, and Bais Rochel took place. Countless yeshiva day schools and high schools were organized or enlarged. And even *kollelim* for post-graduate studies for married scholars came into "style" as a new concept in intensive Torah studies, as initiated in the Lakewood, New Jersey, Beis Medrash Govoha and the Beis Medrash Elyon of Monsey, New York. Torah learning now spread to the farthest corners of the American continent and to Jewish communities far from the main centers of Jewish living and Jewish cultural endeavor.

This Heavenly miracle continues to affect us through the second, mostly American-born generation of Torah scholars and inspired Jewish leaders in the United States and Israel who continue kindling the eternal torch of Torah the world over.

Glossary

AMSHENOVER REBBE: the leader of a Chassidic group originally centered in Amshenov, Poland

CHASSIDIC: of the nature of, or relating to, a movement in Judaism founded by Rabbi Israel Baal Shem Tov, which stressed emotion and enthusiasm along with observance of the Law

CHESSED: lovingkindness (action beyond the letter of the Law)

CHISTKA: a political purge by Communist rulers of "unreliable" elements

CHUMOSH: The Pentateuch (the Five Books of Moses)

COMMISSAR: Communist commissioner

DAYAN: a judge in a rabbinical court

DIASPORA: (Latin for "lands beyond the homeland") the countries of Jewish settlement outside Israel

ESROG: the citrus fruit in the "four species" taken up daily during the SUKKOS festival

GALUS: "exile" — see DIASPORA

GOROL: lot, destiny, fate

GVIR: a rich man

HALACHA (HALACHIC): (pertaining to) normative, definitive Jewish law

HALLEL: psalms of praise and thanksgiving to G-d

HARA-KIRI: a Japanese form of suicide

HAVDALA: the ritual ceremony of farewell at the departure of the Sabbath

INTOURIST: the bureau of internal tourism in the USSR

KIDDUSH: the ritual ceremony of welcoming the Sabbath, recited over a cup of wine

KOLLEL(IM): an academy for the pursuit of advanced Talmudic study.

LUBAVITCHER REBBE: the spiritual leader of the chassidic movement long centered in Lubavitch, White Russia (and with its current headquarters in Brooklyn, New York)

LULOV: the branch of a palm tree — see ESROG

MASHGIACH: the spiritual mentor and guide in a yeshiva, who supervises the study and development of its students

MIKVEH: the place for ritual immersion, either as required by the Law or for spiritual purification

MITZVA: a religious commandment or good deed

NKVD: the "national commissariat of internal affairs," the former title of Russia's Secret Police (K.G.B.)

PALESTINE CERTIFICATE: the special permit to immigrate to Palestine issued to a limited number of Jews by the British mandatory government during its rule of the Jewish Holy Land.

RAV: rabbi

REB: the common, colloquial title of one Jew for another, indicating recognition of a fair degree of status and learning

REB YID: the title one Jew might give another (see REB) when he does not know the other's name

REBBE: a chassidic spiritual leader

ROSH HASHANA: the Jewish New Year

ROSH YESHIVA: the dean of a yeshiva (generally its senior lecturer in Talmud)

SAMURAI: a cast of noble Japanese warriors

SHAILEH: a question involving HALACHA

SHTENDER: a small lectern used by either a student or a teacher in studying Talmud

SHTETL: a small town with a significant observant Jewish population

SHUL: synagogue
SUKKA: "booth": a temporary dwelling roofed by branches or logs, where observant Jews eat and sleep during SUKKOS
SUKKOS: "Tabernacles," the autumn festival that follows ROSH HASHANA and YOM KIPPUR
TALEISIM: four-cornered garments with tassels tied at the corners, worn daily for morning prayer
TALMIDIM: students of TORAH
TALMUD: the multi-volume work of Oral Torah, dating in its present form from ca. 2 BCE to the sixth century CE — the main corpus of study and source of law for observant Jewry.
TORAH: the Written Torah (the biblical text received by Moses) and the Oral Torah, which explains it
TZITZIS: ("tassels" at the corners of) a four-cornered garment worn by Jewish males
TZORAS RABBIM: "a trouble of many" — tribulation that befalls far more than one individual
VA'AD HATZALA: American Jewry's emergency organization, established by its senior Orthodox rabbinate in the war years, for the rescue of the victims of the Nazis
YESHIVA: Torah school, Talmudical academy
YOM KIPPUR: the Day of Atonement, spent in fasting and prayer; the holiest, most solemn day of the Jewish year
YOM TOV: a Jewish festival (or festival day), prescribed by the Torah
YOM TOV SHEINI: a second festival day (immediately following the first), observed outside the Holy Land in accordance with rabbinic decree
ZCHUS: virtue, merit, privilege deserved or bestowed by Heaven

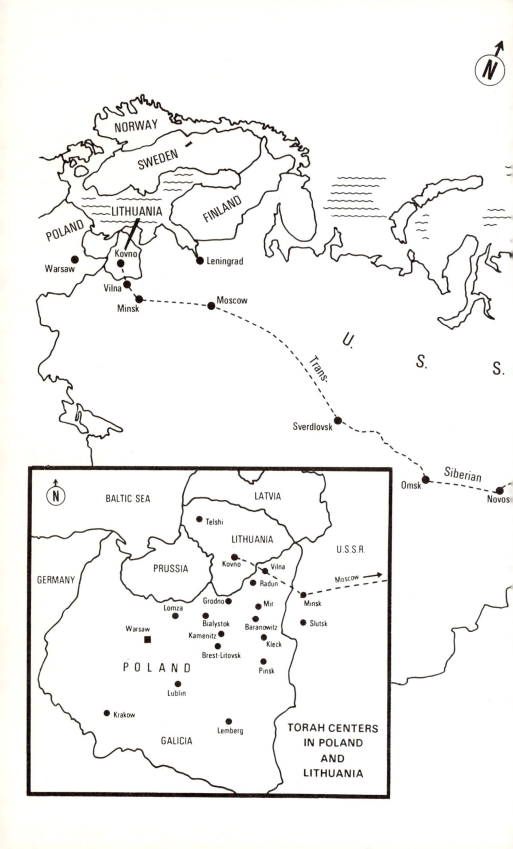

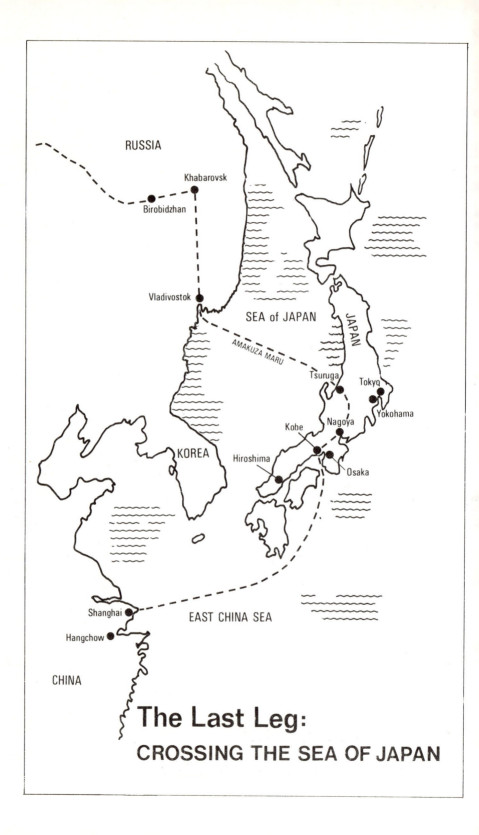

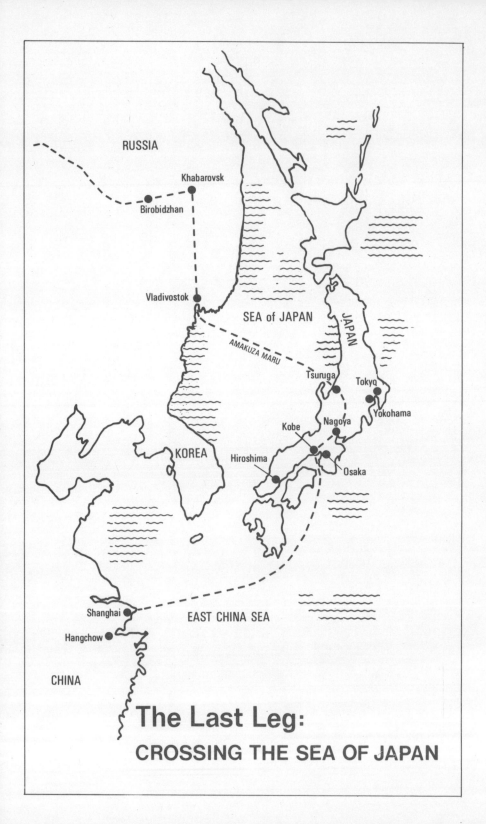